Praise For
Change Your Life Forever

"Change Your Life Forever," is Ronald H. Bartalini's latest book. It is the fourth in a series of doctrinally directed texts designed to enhance our spirituality and to lift, inspire and motivate us to draw closer to God. Written in an easy to follow format, the principles being taught are "forever" based. It was hard to set the book down because it is cleverly intertwined with scriptures, doctrinal explanations, and commentary as well as challenges, which if acted upon, will lead us upward towards the "light" of eternal life.

As I delved deeper into the pages of this pleasantly enlightening text I realized that I still had a ways to go before I am prepared to pass through to eternal life. By reading it you will understand what I mean.

Clark T. Thorstenson, PhD, Emeritus Professor of Administration, BYU, former president, Texas, Huston mission

"Change Your Life Forever," is a fine compendium of wisdom supported by scripture and gospel principles. Ronald H. Bartalini describes a way of life and hope that we all should aspire to. **Riley Moffat, former senior librarian at Joseph F. Smith Library, Brigham Young University-Hawaii**

"Ronald H. Bartalini's latest book, *Change Your Life Forever*, will help anyone who is looking for eternal truths. I highly recommend this book." **Mark Romney, DC**

Change YOUR LIFE Forever

RONALD H. BARTALINI

Sundie Enterprises
Since 1972

Copyright © 2017 by Ronald H. Bartalini
All rights reserved

In accordance with the U.S. Copyright act of 1976, the scanning, uploading, and electronic sharing of any part of this book without the permission of the publisher is unlawful piracy and theft of the author's intellectual property. If you would like to use material from the book (other than for review purposes), prior written permission must be obtained by contacting the publisher at permission:
sundieents@gmail.com

Cover: Painting by Heinrich Hoffmann, 1888 (From Wikipedia, Used By Permission).

ISBN 978-0-9991261-2-7
Library of Congress Control Number
2017909433
Bartalini, Ronald H.

Description

Written as a guide and a roadmap, explaining man's origin and God's plan for man's final destination with easy to follow requirements given by the Savior of the world to enable all of mankind to change their lives for the better forever and return to live with God in heaven once again.

Published by Sundie Enterprises
P.O. Box 1274
Provo, Utah 84603-1274

Change YOUR LIFE Forever

RONALD H. BARTALINI

Contents

Preface	xiii
The ABC's of Permanent Change	35
Chapter A Discover New Ways to Change Your Life	35
Chapter B External Ways We Can Change	47
Chapter C Internal Ways We Can Change	53

Part One

Begin to Change Your Life

1 How to Change for the Better Forever	69
2 How One Young Man- Found God and Changed His Life Forever	76
3 Are You Spiritually Dead?	89
4 How to Recharge- Your Spiritual-Self	92
5 The Light of Christ	96

Part Two

God's Plan for His Children

6 The Origin and Destiny of Man	104
7 The Plan of Salvation	110
8 The Infinite Atonement	114
9 Grace	121

Part Three

Questions All of God's Children Should Answer

10 What Think Ye of Christ?	123
11 Will Christ Still Rescue the Sinner?	126
12 Has the Day of Miracles Ceased?	130

PART FOUR

The Key Players in the Great Drama of Life

13	Who Is God?	135
14	Jesus Christ	140
15	The Holy Ghost	152
16	What Is Man?	154
17	Who Are You?	162
18	Who Is the Adversary?	168

Part Five

Seven Excuses That Could Keep You Out of Heaven

19	I Don't Believe in God	175
20	I Am Not Religious	179
21	I Am Not Worthy	185
22	There Are Too Many Translations of the Bible	190
23	There Are Too Many Churches from Which to Choose	194
24	I Will Follow the Traditions of the Fathers	203
25	I Am Too Old to Change	207

Part Six

The Way to Heaven

26	What Must I Do to Get to Heaven?	211
27	The Gospel of Jesus Christ	227
28	The Book of Mormon	232
29	Faith in Jesus Christ Changes Lives	242

Part Seven

What You Need to Know and Do to Return to Live with God

30	How to Tell If You Have Found the True Church of Jesus Christ	253
31	An Invitation to Come Unto Christ	266
32	Take the Missionary Lessons	270
33	Online Missionaries	273
34	Be Baptized and Receive the Gift of the Holy Ghost	298
	Epilogue	310
	Epilogue #2	316
	About the Author	320
	Index	321

References and Abbreviations

Biblical references are from the King James Version of the Bible. 1 Nephi; 2 Nephi; Jacob; Enos; Mosiah; Alma; Helaman; 3 Nephi; Mormon; Ether and Moroni are books within the Book of Mormon. D&C is an abbreviation for, the Doctrine and Covenants. Moses, Abraham and Joseph Smith 1 and 2 refer to the Book of Moses, the Book of Abraham, and the writings of Joseph Smith and are found within the Pear of Great Price. These works are published by, the Church of Jesus Christ of Latter-day Saints. © by Intellectual Reserve, Inc. All other references are clearly marked within the text.

This material is neither made, provided, approved, nor endorsed by Intellectual Reserve, Inc. or The Church of Jesus Christ of Latter-day Saints. Any content or opinions expressed, implied or included in or with the material are solely those of the owner and not those of Intellectual Reserve, Inc. or The Church of Jesus Christ of Latter-day Saints.

Dedication

For Tommy, Patty and Anita. And for all of God's children, who are serious about changing their lives for the better forever.

Preface

Man did not originate here on earth. Man came from a loftier sphere.

What is it that sets man apart from the animals?

"There is a spirit in man and the inspiration of the Almighty giveth them understanding" (Job 32:8).

From time to time, that spirit within you will nudge you to want to reach upwards to improve your life.

When you feel those gentle nudges, do not deny them.

Chapter A

Discover New Ways to Change Your Life

Are you in the right place? Should you enter into a den of thieves, can you expect to find other than thieves there?

Discover New Ways to Change Your Life

Someone once said, "Nothing good happens after midnight."

On the other hand, if you get up early and go to bed early, it will be much easier to have good things happen to you.

Discover New Ways to Change Your Life

Are you trying to do the right thing?
Are you thinking of others or just yourself?

Are you reading the right books?
When was the last time, you read from the Bible?
Have you ever read the Bible?

Discover New Ways to Change Your Life

When was the last time you prayed? Have you ever prayed?

Have ever prayed and asked God to let you know He exists?

Discover New Ways to Change Your Life

    How can you continue to deny the reality of God if you have never prayed and asked God: to answer you?

So you made a mistake. Are you willing to get up and try again? Experience comes after making many mistakes. Thomas Edison failed 5,000 times before he discovered the correct filament that would conduct electricity. Had he quit trying, the light bulb would have had to wait for someone else to discover it. Who knows how much longer we would have had to wait to replace candles and kerosene lamps?

Discover New Ways to Change Your Life

There are no perfect people in this world. Everyone makes mistakes. That is why we have erasers.

Everyone is still learning. That is why we have schools, teachers and books to read.

I visited a friend several years following moving to another state. When I returned to visit him, he was doing the exact same thing as when I left him. It was almost as if I was in a time warp. Nothing had changed. The old, bad habits were still being practiced even at the same hour of the day.

God does not want you to stay the same year after year. God does not want you to remain neutral.

We read from the book of Revelation:
"I know thy works, that thou art neither cold not hot: I would that thou wert cold or hot.
So then because thou art lukewarm, and neither cold nor hot, I will spue thee out of my mouth" (Revelation 3:15-16).

I visited another friend in a different state and he was now doing something new that had improved his life. God wants you to get better every year. From His transcendent Sermon on the Mount, Jesus taught:

"Be ye therefore perfect, even as your Father which is in heaven is perfect" (Matthew 5:48).

We will not reach perfection in this life and we will not attain perfection without inviting Christ into our life. But if we do, and we imagine the Savior walking next to us as he did those men on their way to Emmaus, suddenly our life will take on a new meaning. Our life will now be filled with confidence, peace and the understanding that we are on the right path and walking the right way. For he said: "I am the way, the truth, and the life" (John 14:6).

Discover New Ways to Change Your Life

You cannot expect your life to change for the better if you keep on doing the same things.

When I was seventeen I discovered Benjamin Franklin's autobiography wherein he lists thirteen virtues, which he intended to master. He created a chart to keep track of his progress. Rather than record Franklin's thirteen virtues here, I commend his work to you for your own discovery.

I will instead give you my own list of virtues to make a part of your life:

First: Do not boast of your own accomplishments. Let another man's lips praise thee, and not thy own.

Second: Do not lie. Do not even tell half-truths and do not deceive. Speak only the truth and nothing but the truth.

Third: Do not speak ill of thy neighbor. If you do not have something good to say about someone, do not speak.

Fourth: Do not gossip. Do not find fault with others.

Fifth: When you speak of others, always find something good to say about them.

Sixth: Be the person that others will call on to ask for help.

Seventh: When you agree to do something, do not defer to do it.

Eight: Do not just be on time. Be fifteen minutes early to all, important meetings.

Ninth: Say, thank you often. Learn to say thank you in many languages. Those two words will open more doors than a master key.

Tenth: Do not judge others.
You do not know why people do what they do.
Eleventh: Be forgiving. Ask forgiveness of those you have offended. Forgive those who have offended you. Have the courage to forgive yourself. That will allow God to forgive you.
Twelfth: Be generous with what you have. Give to him that asketh of thee but beyond that, be discerning to see thy brother in need that you might offer your help before you are asked.
Thirteenth: Trust in the Lord with all thine heart; and lean not to thy own understanding. In all thy ways acknowledge him, and he shall direct thy paths. (Proverbs 3:5-6).

Keep a chart of your progress. Record dates with details of each event. When you look back on your chart one or two years later, you will be amazed at the improvements you have made.

Perhaps even more important than a list of virtues to master will be, coming to know yourself. You will do well to know your own strengths and weaknesses. It will be pretty hard for you to improve yourself if you don't know what areas of your life you need improvement. Ask your spouse. Ask your best friends. Ask someone who will tell you the truth and not what you want to hear. You may be doing something that is offensive to others that you are completely unaware of. Isn't it time you found out what your strengths and weaknesses are?

Discover New Ways to Change Your Life

    Permanent change is a process.
Human beings do not change in a day.
It takes time, even a lifetime.

A good way to begin is by taking small steps. Children learn to ride a bicycle by first using training wheels. Don't put the cart before the horse. Win one small victory at a time. Soon, there will be many small victories won.

Discover New Ways to Change Your Life

What character trait will you choose to work on to improve your life?

You may choose swearing and using off color language. That choice may cause you to go back to church.

Discover New Ways to Change Your Life

    Once you have done that, you may choose to stop speaking unkindly about your neighbors. That decision will definitely allow you to have more friends.

The smallest act of kindness will do more to impact your life positively and cause a permanent change in who you are and who you can become than almost anything else you could do.

Many small acts of kindness over time, will allow you to become a new you.

Discover New Ways to Change Your Life

    There are many things you can do to improve the lives of others. For example: Taking a neighbor to a doctor's appointment. Raking the leaves from your neighbor's front lawn. Shoveling snow from your neighbor's front porch, sidewalk and driveway. Visiting a neighbor who is sick. Bringing a home cooked meal to a shut in.

Set aside some time each day to improve your own life.

Discover New Ways to Change Your Life

    Set aside additional time each day to help others with small acts of kindness.

Something as simple as a smile, a clasp of the hands, a pat on the back, can work wonders in both you: the giver, and the other fella, the receiver.

We are all given 24 hours in each day to live our lives. However, life does not go on forever.

When will your end come? No man knows how much time he has to live. God gave King Hezekiah 15 additional years to live. (Isaiah 38:1-5). It will probably not be so with us.

Adam lived 930 years. (Genesis 5:5). Noah lived 950 years. (Genesis 9:29). Abraham lived 175 years. (Genesis 25:7-8). Moses lived 120 years. Deuteronomy 34:7). According to data compiled by the Social Security Administration:

"A man reaching age 65 in the year (2016) can expect to live, on average, until age 84.3. A woman turning age 65 today can expect to live, on average, until age 86.6. And those are just averages. About one out of every four 65-year-olds today will live past age 90, and one out of 10 will live past age 95."

We can all learn to make better use of our time to improve our own lives and the lives of others.

The best way I know to do this is by prioritizing each and every thing you do. This is what has helped me: "Put God first in all things and give all the honor and glory to God."

By this I mean, if your list of things to do in a day includes going to the Post Office, paying bills, picking up groceries, running the children to school, driving to work and any number of other things, (Try getting up a little bit earlier to leave time to put God first before the cares of the world, begin).

An additional example would be listing the things we do that are mostly, a waste of time. Watching TV for hours, for example. I gave up television watching more than ten years ago and my life has been better for it. Young people may wish to cut back on social media and video games.

This deceptively simple adjustment of prioritizing will work wonders in improving your life and allowing you to, Change Your Life Forever.

Chapter B

External Ways We Can Change

Decide to Change

Your journey can begin the moment you decide it is time to change your life for the better forever. Housewives clean their homes. Men maintain their vehicles by periodically changing the oil and lubricating them. Changing your life forever will require you to clean your spiritual house. Jesus had something to say about this: "When the unclean spirit is gone out of a man, he walketh through dry places, seeking rest; and finding none, he saith, I will return unto my house whence I came out. And when he cometh, he findeth it swept and garnished. Then goeth he, and taketh to him seven other spirits more wicked than himself; and they enter in, and dwell there: and the last state of that man is worse than the first" (Luke 11:24-26).

This suggests that as we are cleaning up our lives, we should be ever vigilant and not forget to invite the Savior to keep us and protect us from evil. The sure way to do this is to continue to keep God's commandments and endure until the end. Should we make a mistake, let us take heart that because of the atonement of Jesus Christ, we can repent of our misgivings.

Man is not just a physical or natural being. The Father of us all made us first spiritually in heaven. We are therefore both a spiritual and a physical being. It is the spiritual part of man that we must focus on to effect permanent change.

The things of God are spiritual and they must be spiritually discerned. The natural man does not understand the things of God. God must be understood spiritually. "But the natural man receiveth not the things of the Spirit of God: for they are foolishness unto him: neither can he know them, because they are spiritually discerned" (1 Corinthians 2:14).

Set a Goal

You may not get it right the first time. You must be willing to make mistakes. Allow yourself to make mistakes. Flesh it out. Remember, the thing you do over and over gets easier each time you do it. If no one made mistakes there would be no erasers. There would be no editors. Be the editor not just of those words you may write, be the editor of your own life.

Report Back to Yourself

If you get into the habit of setting goals without reporting back to yourself and therefore keeping careful and meticulous records such as your own captain's log, undoubtedly, the following will happen: Your goals will be like that kite floating with the wind because someone has let go of their kite string. Your kite will soar wherever the wind takes it and will eventually probably end up in the kite-eating tree. On the other hand, if you report back to yourself every day and keep your own captain's log with careful and meticulous records you will find that doing so will reinforce your desire to succeed.

Be Positive & Thank the Naysayers

Instead of listening to and believing the

naysayers; thank them, and consider them God's gift to you. The naysayers represent everything that is negative but if you consider that they are sent by God to inspire you to conquer any and all obstacles, you may wish to thank them all.

If you are really on to something good, something that will help make the world a better place in which to live, there will be many naysayers who will say, "It can't be done," "You can't do that," or my personal favorite, "That is impossible!" I just love it when people tell me that what I want to do is impossible because that just makes me want to do it even more.

These folks are forgetting, "All things are possible with Christ." Jesus said, "If thou canst believe, all things are possible to him that believeth" (Mark 9:23). The Savior also taught, "If you have faith as a grain of mustard seed, you shall say unto this mountain, Remove hence to yonder place, and it shall remove; and nothing shall be impossible to you" (Matthew 17:20).

The Things We Resist

Often the things we resist are the very things that are good for us and will improve our lives the most. Gene Autry resisted recording "Rudolph the Red Nosed Reindeer" until his wife finally persuaded him that children would love the song.

"Gene Autry's recording of Rudolph the Red Nosed Reindeer sold 1.75 million copies its first Christmas season, eventually selling a total of 12.5 million. Cover versions included, sales exceed 150 million copies, second only to Bing Crosby's "White Christmas." (From Wikipedia).

This is a pretty good reason to listen to your wife or a friend who is trying to advise you to not resist that which could be good for you.

Excuses

There must be hundreds upon hundreds of excuses not the least of which are: "I don't have enough time. I don't have enough money." In the end, all they are after all, is just that, excuses. I like that which I learned in the Civil Air Patrol when I was fifteen years old, I was taught, "No excuse Sir!" That has stayed with me all these years. You will find that if you defer from making excuses you will learn something brand new about personal integrity. Among many other truths you will learn is this: doing what you are asked to do and doing what you say you will do, creates your personal integrity. Nothing is more important than your integrity for without it, you are just another person in a sea of people who may be living but are not yet worthy of being trusted. It is greater to be trusted than to be loved.

Chapter C

Internal Ways to Change

Do Not Judge Others

Is there a difference between wishing to lift others up and finding faults or criticizing them? Yes. Everything depends upon the desire and intent of your heart. Are you just criticizing or do you wish to lift the other person up and allow them to become better? You are the only one who can answer those questions. Be certain to answer honestly because you may find that you are guilty of only judging others.

This Is Huge!

Judging others, and criticizing others just to find faults with them to make you feel superior to them will backfire. This behavior will literally hold back blessings that could be coming your way. Understanding how quickly this behavior can limit you from receiving blessings and curtail your spiritual progression is huge! Don't get caught up in this habit pattern because it will absolutely stunt your spiritual growth.

Change Your Thoughts

Did you know that you can only think of one thing at a time? God is teaching man to slow down and live in the moment. So many people are rushing here and there and everywhere but they seldom stop to slow down and enjoy the wonder of each day. Like an engine that needs energy to function, man needs good clean, uplifting and pure thoughts to keep his spiritual self running and getting closer to God.

One proven way to do this is to search the scriptures. The Holy scriptures-are the word of God. They are God's instructions to man to show

Internal Ways to Change

man how to change his life for the better forever! For example, consider this verse:

"Commit thy works unto the Lord and thy thoughts shall be established" (Proverbs 15:3).

Why not take some time out every day to lose yourself in the scriptures. I promise you if you do, your life will begin to change for the better forever. The scriptures are helpful in explaining the power of our thoughts: "For as he thinketh in his heart, so is he" (Proverbs 23:7).

"For out of the abundance of the heart the mouth speaketh" (Proverbs 4:23).

The following scripture teaches us that God's thoughts are connected to his ways, and so it is with man. A man's thoughts will determine what a man does.

Look at these words carefully:

"For my thoughts are not your thoughts neither are my ways your ways. For as the heavens are higher than the earth so are my ways higher than your ways and my thoughts than your thoughts" (Isaiah 55:8-9).

Behavior to Check Concerning Yourself

Check yourself for the language you use when speaking to others. For example, do you find yourself saying, "*stay out of trouble.*" This little quip although probably meant to just be friendly conversation does not uplift and inspire the person hearing it to do good things. On the contrary, it comes across as a suggestion that the person hearing this statement must be especially watchful because you suspect him to easily find his way into trouble. Please remove these sentiments from your conversations with others. Here is another phrase to strike from your language. It is not only non productive it comes across almost as an indictment of guilt. Stop saying, "If we can trust him," or "I'm not sure he or she can be trusted." Some folks are insensitive enough to speak these words in the presence of the person in question. People who say this to others about another person are probably not very trustworthy themselves.

    One of my favorite infractions follows. This little saying has become a permanent part of our language in America today. I hear it spoken everywhere and by people of all ages and backgrounds. Here it is, "good luck." Although the people who say this to others probably mean well, hearing these words spoken does not uplift and inspire one to do good or to succeed. It would be much better to say, "May the Lord bless you, or "Blessings to you," or "Keep on believing, work hard and all will be well with you."

Internal Ways to Change

Decide That You Will Succeed

No matter how many times you have to fail to get it right, decide that you will not quit. We can all become master practitioners and splendid examples of living the second great commandment. When we concern ourselves with serving and ministering to the needs of others just as the Savior did during his mortal ministry our lives will change dramatically and permanently. Serving others can be contagious.

Be the Person Who Others Ask for Help

"Give to him that asketh of thee and from him that would borrow of thee, turn not thou away" (Matthew 5:42).

"Give freely to the poor when thou hast it by thee" (Proverbs 3:28).

Before anyone will ever ask you for help you will have to first earn that person's trust and confidence. How do you do that? Be certain not to ever refuse giving your help when it is within your power to do so. Don't say, "Tomorrow I will help," when you know you can help today. Don't refuse to help and then make up an excuse that the other person can see is flimsy or even an outright lie. If you cannot help and you do have an honest reason why, simply say, "I cannot help now." But be sure to always help when you can and even volunteer your help and resources whenever you can. The worst thing you could possibly do is to say you will help and agree to do so and to show up at a given time and then fail to show up at all. It is good to help when you are asked but far better to help before you are asked.

      Perhaps if we consider that everything we have is not ours at all but we are simply the caretakers of what God has blessed us with, giving to others will become more palatable. Consider also that for some, asking another for help may not be the easiest thing for them to do. We would all like to think that the other fella should be able to take care of himself. But unless you also one day become that other fella who finds himself needing help and needing to ask for help you will probably never understand how hard asking for it might be.

      There is this little matter of not pride but dignity and human beings like to think they can maintain a modicum of it. You might also consider that God may be testing you, when you see someone standing on the street holding up a sign and asking for help. If you ever look into the eyes of someone holding up a sign and asking for help please consider this. That person could be one of God's angels testing you. Look into their eyes and you may get your own answer. The question now is, what will you do? Will you help them or will you drive away. The human reaction will be, to judge them. You may think, they brought this upon themselves. They are a professional panhandler or I don't have time for this now, I'll help on another day.

But use your own common sense. Perhaps say a little prayer and ask God to give you the answer but remember, it is not our job to judge another but to be merciful and to forgive all men and women as we have hope our Father in heaven will forgive us.

Lift People Up

How do you do that?

Compliments

A sincere compliment can work wonders in building another's confidence. Doing this must be learned it cannot be just thrown out there. If it is, it will be received as insincere, phony and fake, in other words, meaningless. For example,

"I really like your dress Jane. I especially like the details on the fringe work. I can see that the sewing was done by, a meticulous professional. The color compliments you eyes and makes you stand out in a crowd."

Now consider this compliment by comparison. "Yo, Jane. Nice dress." This person might have also added, "My mother told me to say that." Even so, when someone does pay you a compliment, be certain to thank them. They may be perfectly sincere but just do not know how to express themselves yet.

Build People Up

This is also an asset that must be learned. To be a success at building people up requires some homework and research on your part. You will have to invest some time in truly getting to know someone before you can accomplish this.

For example, you can begin by letting people talk about themselves. When the opportunity presents itself you may ask them, "What new projects are you working on these days?" Should they be involved in trying to do their part in making the world a better place in which to live by trying to discover a cure for cancer or visiting terminally ill children, they will want to talk about that.

Not everyone will be doing this, so whatever it is they are doing, encourage them to talk about it and as they do you can encourage them to continue to reach their goals. It will never cease to amaze me how effective a little encouragement can be. When someone reaches a goal they have worked on for long months or even years, it will then be time for some hearty praise and approbation. In the meantime, a simple pat on the back and such words as "keep up the good work, I believe in you and I'm sure you can do it," will also work wonders.

I often wonder how many great works of art, and discoveries of science would have never happened if there were no one who encouraged, and believed in those who made those great works of art or did the discovering.

Make Him Better

Just how do you go about making someone better? You do not do this by never learning anyone's name. You do not do this by never smiling and saying hello and asking people how they are doing and how their day is going? You do not do this by not first being an example of living a good life and trying to emulate our great exemplar even Jesus Christ.

You do accomplish making someone

better by truly caring about all of God's children. When you do, you will notice little things about others that can be improved. Now comes the hard part. How do you suggest an improvement in another without giving offense? I do not believe this can be done without God's help.

    To begin you will have to wait for the right moment. Timing is just as important as the words you will speak. When the moment is right, you will know and only then will you be effective in trying to make someone better. You will want to do this when you and the other individual are alone and away from and out of the hearing distance of others. Even then if will be wise to whisper the words you must be impressed by the spirit of the Lord to speak. You must be certain that you are doing any correcting in the spirit of love and so you will want to compliment the person by speaking the most sincere words you can find about how much you appreciate this person's service and mention other good points the person may have.

    Now comes the delicate part. If there is something they are doing that is not appropriate or that does not inspire to lift others up simply explain to them what it is they are doing and if you do this in the spirit of love, if you respect the other person's feelings being careful not to criticize but explain that you are doing this to lift him up and to make him better, all will be well.

Internal Ways to Change

Invite Correction

Are you nuts? Why would I possibly want to do that? I am sure you would not if you wish to stay the same and not improve your spiritual self. But if you would truly like to change your spiritual self and progress spiritually you will one day discover that reproof and correction is how we grow spiritually!

Consider the words of one of God's servants who was known as the wisest man on earth during his lifetime. The prophet Solomon has given us this proverb: "For whom the Lord loveth he correcteth; even as a father the son in whom he delighteth" (Proverbs 3:12).

Therefore, if you are being corrected from time to time God must love you a lot. Knowing this, there are some who invite correction and always express their gratitude and appreciation for it when it comes. Then there are others who always seem to feel picked on when they are corrected and they never say, "thank you," having received any kind of correction.

An Attitude Adjustment Is Required

Be grateful for everything, even the air you

breathe. A grateful heart is a forgiving heart and such a person will be in good stead with God. God has made everything. God has made everywhere. Be thankful for your life and all that you have been given. Begin saying, "Thank you" many times each day and this small change or adjustment in your attitude will not only determine your altitude, it will begin to permanently change your life positively! The recorded phone message from our public library says, "Thank you for letting us serve you." The local Veterans administration has a similar message when you call them. It says, "Thank you for your service."

I believe these organizations are on to something. When was the last time you heard yourself say, "Thank you" to someone for anything?

Say Thank You Three Times Each Day
Keep a Record of It

Saying "thank you" three times each day, for three weeks and keeping a record of it and then reading your log back to yourself at night and on each following morning, may seem like a simple thing but it is not at all. This

Internal Ways to Change

deceptively simple activity could be the beginning of changing your life forever!

Saying "thank you" demonstrates that one has a sense of civility and respect for others. Saying please and thank you is evidence that one has good manners. But the words, "thank you," are evidence of something even more far reaching. Saying "thank you" often, with sincerity shows the world that you have a sense of gratitude. A grateful heart is a loving heart and one who loves is of God. Jesus said, "By this ye shall all men know that ye are my disciples, if ye have love one to another" (John 13:35).

Since we are now in the month of December for the year 2016, I decided to take a look at my own log for this year. When I finished reading it, I then went back and read my records for the two previous years. I was amazed at how much I had forgotten that took place as the years went by. This helped me to also remember just how many times the Lord blesses us throughout our lives.

Jesus made a point of teaching us about the importance of saying, "Thank you" during his mortal ministry: "And it came to pass, as he went to Jerusalem, that he passed through the midst of Samaria and Galilee. And as he entered into a certain village, there met him ten men that were lepers, which stood afar off; And they lifted up their voices, and said, Jesus, Master, have mercy on us. And when he saw them, he said unto them,

Go show yourselves unto the priests. And it came to pass, that, as they went, they were cleansed. And one of them, when he saw that he was healed, turned back, and with a loud voice glorified God, *And fell down, on his face at his feet, giving him thanks: and he was a Samaritan.* And Jesus answering said, "Were there not ten cleansed? but where are the nine? There are not found that returned to give glory to God, save this stranger. And he said unto him, Arise, go thy way: Thy faith had made thee whole" (Luke 17:11-19).

Learn People's Names and Use Them

If you add one other ingredient to this ongoing recipe for success, you will find even more favor with man. People like to hear their names spoken. Some are so fond of their names that they wear them as nametags on their person. Others have their names on T-shirts and baseball caps. So called celebrities seem like they can never get enough of hearing their names and seeing their images displayed all over social media. If you are wise enough to learn the names of those you come in contact with and use them each time you see them, you will begin to notice that things in your life will change in a positive way.

Internal Ways to Change

Acknowledge God's Hand in Everything

The man or woman who believes they can get through life all by themselves and without God will certainly be able to do so and even achieve a great many successes. There are many millionaires, even billionaires, Academy Award, Olympic Gold Medal, and Nobel Prize winners. There are many great artists, inventors and men and women who have achieved many honors and titles in this life all on their own. However, when they leave this life not only do their riches stay behind but so does their fame, honors, and titles. "You can't take it with you when you die," was never more powerfully enforced than upon those who do not acknowledge God in all things.

Why is this so? If it is alive and has a spirit, God made it. Why? Because Jesus Christ made everything and everything that is alive was first created spiritually in heaven by his Father before it was created on the earth.

That which gives life to everything is the light of Christ for without this life giving light there is no life! Therefore, we should acknowledge the hand of God in everything. Because if it is alive; Jesus Christ made it. John the Beloved has said of the Son of God, "All things were made by him; and without him was not anything made that was made" (John 1:3). That pretty much sums it up. If Jesus made everything surely we should acknowledge the reality that he is aware of everything he has made. We would all do well to thank our Father in Heaven and his beloved Son for all they have given us and for all the blessings we will continue to receive as we keep God's commandments and endeavor to endure until the end.

Chapter One

How to Change Your Life Forever

Have you had a mighty change of heart? Has the look on your countenance changed? Is there a light that now shines more brightly from behind your eyes? Have the desires of your heart changed? Do you now desire to do only good continually and do you no longer have an inclination to do evil? Only God can change a man that way. Only God can give a man a new heart.

Only God can change a man for the better forever!

We are here on earth to see whether we will keep God's commandments or not. Your conscience is spinning with that reality. If you miss that salient truth, you are missing a big part of the meaning of life!

Change is a natural, physical or human idea. Change for the better is getting closer to a spiritual idea but it is still very human because most all change for the better is temporary. There is one notable exception, "Whatever principle of intelligence we attain unto in this life, will rise with us in the resurrection. And if a person gains more knowledge and intelligence in this life through his diligence and obedience than another, he will have so much the advantage in the world to come" (D&C 130: 18-19).

Change for the better forever is a spiritual idea because that defines the mission of God for you. What is God the Eternal Father's mission statement for you? "This is my work and my glory, to bring to pass the immortality and eternal life of man" (Moses 1:39).

To change your moral compass requires changing your spirituality for the better forever. God made you. Before the earth was formed God made the spirit bodies of everyone who will eventually live on the earth. When the earth was formed God then made man from the dust of the earth and breathed the breath of life into man's nostrils and man became a living soul. God made you in his own image and likeness.

God loves you. You do not have to do

anything for God to love you. God has always loved you unconditionally. God wants you back in heaven again to live with him forever. When you stand before God in a resurrected, perfected and glorified body that you might endure the glory of God and look into our beloved heavenly Father's eyes and God takes you in his arms and holds you close, you will understand God's love for you is greater than anything you have ever experienced on this earth.

God wants you to change for the better forever. A great definition for the phrase: change for the better forever is the word, *repentance*. Change comes through faith in Christ unto repentance, "which faith and repentance bringeth a change of heart to them" (Helaman 15:7).

One of the most powerful sermons we have in all of recorded scripture is found in the fifth chapter of Alma within the Book Of Mormon. I can still remember the branch president of our tiny branch in Fredericton, New Brunswick reading the entire sermon to the branch during a Sacrament meeting when I was a young missionary serving there. It is just over five pages long and I commend it to you to read often. In his sermon, Alma the younger asks some very good questions. These are questions we should ask ourselves at least once each year to check our personal eternal progress: "And now behold, I ask of you, my brethren of the church, *have ye spiritually been born of God? Have ye received his image in your countenances? Have ye experienced this mighty change in your hearts?*

Do ye exercise faith in the redemption of him who created you? Do you look forward with an eye of faith, and view this mortal body raised in immortality, and this corruption raised in incorruption, to stand before God to be judged according to the deeds which have been done in the mortal body" (Alma 5: 14-15)?

"I speak by way of command unto you that belong to the church; *and unto those who do not belong to the church I speak by way of invitation, saying: Come and be baptized unto repentance, that ye also may be partakers of the fruit of the tree of life*" (Alma 5: 62).

If you want to change for the better forever, you will need Jesus Christ in you life. Jesus is in the forever business. Every thing Christ does lasts forever. The good news is, Jesus is standing at your proverbial front door and knocking right now and waiting for you to hear him and let him into your heart and into your life. Jesus Christ can change your heart and give you a new heart and a new life, if you will let him. Jesus has the answer to every question you will ever ask.

How to Change Your Life Forever

What should you do when you let Christ into your life? The voice of our lord and Savior came into the heart and mind of a Book of Mormon prophet long ago with the answer:

And the Father said: Repent ye repent ye, and be baptized in the name of my Beloved Son. And also, the voice of the Son came unto me, saying: He that is baptized in my name, to him will the Father give the Holy Ghost, like unto me; wherefore, follow me, and do the things which ye have seen me do" (2 Nephi 31:5-12).

"Wherefore, do the things which I have told you I have seen that your Lord and Your Redeemer should do; for, for this cause have they been shown unto me, that ye might know the gate by which ye should enter. *For the gate by which ye should enter is repentance and baptism by water; and then cometh a remission of your sins by fire and by the Holy Ghost.* And then are ye in this straight and narrow path which leads to eternal life; yea, ye have entered in by the gate; ye have done according to the commandments of the Father and the Son; and ye have received the Holy Ghost, which witnesses of the Father and the Son, unto the fulfilling of the promise which he hath made, that if ye entered in by the way ye should receive.

And now, my beloved brethren, after ye have gotten into this straight and narrow path, I would ask if all is done? Behold, I say unto you

Nay; for ye have not come thus far save it were by the word of Christ with unshaken faith in him, relying wholly upon the merits of him who is mighty to save.

Wherefore, ye must press forward with a steadfastness in Christ, having a perfect brightness of hope, and a love of God and of all men. Wherefore, if ye shall press forward, feasting upon the word of Christ, and endure to the end, behold, thus saith the Father: Ye shall have eternal life.

And now, behold, my beloved brethren, this is the way; and there is none other way nor name given under heaven whereby man can be saved in the kingdom of God. And now behold, this is the doctrine of Christ, and the only and true doctrine of the Father, and of the Son, and of the Holy Ghost, which is one God, without end. Amen" (2 Nephi 31: 17-21).

"For behold, again I say unto you that if ye will enter in by the way, and receive the Holy Ghost, it will show unto you all things what ye should do. Behold, this is the doctrine of Christ, and there will be no more doctrine given until after he shall manifest himself unto you in the flesh. And when he shall manifest himself unto you in the flesh, the things he shall say unto you shall ye observe to do" (2 Nephi 32: 5-6).

From the first man Adam until the ministry of Jesus Christ and from the ministry of Jesus Christ until today, the steps required to change for the better forever have remained the same. They are: faith in the Lord Jesus Christ, which leads to repentance, then comes baptism for the remission of sins, then comes the gift of the Holy Ghost, and then one must endure until the end.

      You have just read about the doctrine of Christ. You will discover the same requirements in the Father's Plan of Salvation (see Chapter Eight) and in the gospel of Jesus Christ (see Chapter Twenty-Two). This is the pattern. These are the steps required to enter the kingdom of God. There is no other way. There is no other name given whereby men may be saved other than, Jesus Christ. As you read, you will discover that faith in Jesus Christ, the light of Christ, the Holy Ghost, the atonement of Jesus Christ and the grace of Christ are all connected and work in harmony to allow us to Change for The Better Forever which is another way of saying: to return to live with God forever.

Chapter Two

How One Young Man Found God and Changed His Life Forever

No man has ever found God without the Holy Ghost. The mission of the Holy Ghost is to bear witness to the world that God the Eternal Father lives and that Jesus is the Christ. The Holy Ghost whispers to man that Jesus Christ is the only name given under heaven whereby men may be saved. (Acts 4:12). The still small voice of the Holy Ghost whispers to all men and women that these things are true. Man must simply learn how to listen in order that he might hear the Holy Ghost speak to him in his own mind and in his own heart.

How One Young Man Found God and Changed His Life Forever

God has given man the Holy Ghost that man might be able to remember living with God in heaven. Jesus said: "But the Comforter, which is the Holy Ghost, whom the Father will send in my name, he shall teach you all things *and bring all things to your remembrance, whatsoever I have said unto you*" (John 14:26). The Holy Ghost helps all men believe in Christ and desire to do good works while they live on the earth. The Holy Ghost is a member of the Godhead. The Holy Ghost is a spirit personage in the form of a man. The Holy Ghost can descend upon a man a not tarry with him. (See D&C 130: 22-23). The personage which is the Holy Ghost can only be in one place at a time but the power and influence of the Holy Ghost can be felt everywhere throughout all of time and space. When a man feels the power and influence of the Holy Ghost, that feeling will be something he has never felt before. That feeling cannot be imitated by man or by the devil. When a man has an experience with the Holy Ghost, that man's life will change for the better forever! The Holy Ghost usually speaks to men by communicating in an inaudible, still, small voice, which can only be heard with a person's heart and mind and not by his ears. Therefore, man must recalibrate his capacity to listen that he might learn to hear the Holy Ghost speak to him. The following song was written for the album, *Gravity* and it may help you learn to listen:

Learn to Listen
Copyright © 2017 by Ron Bartalini
From the Album, Gravity/Ron Bartalini

You have got to... listen without using your ears.
You have got to.... see by only using your heart.
You can learn to.... feel everything--- in a way
that you're not used to---
That's the only way to the stars. Repeat...

Now the universe, it doesn't like fear no... so you
can no longer be afraid...
And the elements...they want you to believe...
yeah....
If you're gonna walk on water...
You've got to chase your doubts away.

You've got to listen without using your ears.
You've got to see by only using your heart.
You've got to feel everything in a way that you're
not used to.
That's the only way to the stars.
Now the people all around you... they're gonna
say you're nuts.
They will all say... you're crazy as a loon.
But you don't pay attention to their convention
You just keep reaching far beyond the moon...
You've got to... listen without using your ears.

How One Young Man Found God and Changed His Life Forever

You've to... see by only using your heart.
You've to... feel everything in a way you're not used to...
That's the only way to the stars.
You've got to listen.

Learn to listen.
You've got to listen.
Learn to listen.
Listen...learn to listen. Be still...and know He is there.

  I was in the grocery store just a few days ago and there was a mother with a shopping cart behind me at one of the self-serve check out stations. She had more than one child with her. All at once, a little boy standing up in her shopping cart said, "Mom, I'm begging you, get me a donut!" Then he proceeded to say, "I want a donut! I want a donut! I want a donut, about seven more times.
  Thinking I might calm the little boy down and thereby help his mother, I walked over to the little fella in the grocery cart and looked deeply into his eyes and asked him, "Do you know Homer Simpson? Homer has lots of donuts." All I got back from the little guy was a blank stare. But later that day, I realized that little boy did teach me something.
  If you will pray to God with the same

intensity and focus of the little boy who wanted a donut, you will get an answer from God. If you can say, "God, I'm begging you, please reveal yourself to me. Please, let me know you live. Please, let me know you do exist!" If you can pray that prayer sincerely and with the intensity and real intent of the little boy who wanted a donut, you will get your answer from God.

Let us take another look at the prayers of Enos. The day came when Enos wanted to know if God lives. Enos has recorded his story for us in the Of Mormon. Enos said: "I will tell you of the wrestle which I had before God, before I received a remission of my sins. Behold, I went to hunt beasts in the forests; and the words which I had often heard my father speak concerning eternal life, and the joy of the saints, sunk deep into my heart.

And my soul hungered; and I kneeled down before my Maker, and I cried unto him in mighty prayer and supplication for mine own soul; and all the day long did I cry unto him; yea, and when the night came I did still raise my voice high that it reached the heavens" (Enos verses 1-4).

Enos said, *"my soul hungered,"* not for a donut but to be able to find God and to save his own soul. Enos was consistent and faithful. He did not quit. Enos kept on praying. Enos prayed all day and into the night.

How One Young Man Found God and Changed His Life Forever

Enos was focused. Enos stayed on point. Enos did not utter a haphazard and insincere prayer. Enos wanted to know. Enos prayed with real intent. Enos tells us: "And there came a voice unto me, saying; Enos, thy sins are forgiven thee, and thou shalt be blessed. And I, Enos, knew that God could not lie, Wherefore, my guilt was swept away. And I said, Lord, how is it done? And he said unto me: Because of thy faith in Christ whom thou hast never before heard nor seen. And many years pass away before he shall manifest himself in the flesh" (Enos, verses 7-8).

Now here is the story of a young man who was born in Beijing, China. This young man found God when he was fourteen years old which is the same age Joseph Smith was when he found God. Elder Guo is now serving as a full-time missionary in my small city in Utah. I have only done a small amount of editing his story because changing his words would certainly take away from the power of his testimony.

Elder Guo's Conversion Story

I was born and raised in Beijing, China where I did not have many religious freedom or Christian churches. By the influence of our culture and government, I was taught since I was young that there is no God, or he was already dead. For these, variety of reasons, I had never heard about God neither Christ before. The only basic religion I had touched was Buddhism, I went to Buddhism temple three times a year regularly and that is all.

About six years ago, I met a friend accidentally at our house because we had a dinner party together. Lots of people showed up. It's close to 20 people so that I couldn't remember all of their faces. However, one of them left a strong impression on me because he was the only person didn't drink beer, coffee or tea among all of these people, I was amazed and wondering about why?

After a while, I was encouraged to ask him why you don't drink these beverages? I said, "You don't like it or are you allergic to these drinks?" He answered with a smiling face and said to me that he couldn't tell me, because of some policies. I had never heard this answer before so it made me more curious. I was pondering throughout the entire time, what is the policy? Why couldn't he tell me? After the dinner, I couldn't extinguish my curiosity so I talked to him again at a corner that only we were there.

I asked him with a sincere heart: "I think you are so different than others, you must have something special that you haven't told me yet.

How One Young Man Found God and Changed His Life Forever

Is that correct?" He smiled again and answered my question with this special answer I will never ever forget: "My friend, I'm a member of the LDS church, I can't tell you because the Chinese government doesn't allow me to do it but we believe in Christ and we believe don't drink coffee, beer or tea is a Christ's commandment."

That's the first time in my life I heard Christ's name, first time witnessed a real Christian member. First time I saw a church that truly exercise their beliefs and keep their standards. First time felt so close to the light I was searching for. I calmed down and asked with uncertainty; "Can you teach me? I really want to learn." Then, by the power of the spirit, he felt strong promptings that he should give me his only Book of Mormon that he holds every single day. He passed it to me and promised me that If I read it sincerely with a real intent, I will find answers from it even though no one is gonna help me."

I took his advise-and began my journey. I started to read it when I was 14, I put it under my bed, so I can read it every single day. However, I didn't really understand the Book of Mormon for close to five months, I felt 1 Nephi, 2 Nephi, Alma, Mosiah, all of these chapters are just like historic stories, not records of God. I thought about giving up, because I don't understand why I have to read a book that I don't even understand. But whenever I thought about this, the promise my friend gave to me just pumped into my head. So I kept going.

2010, January 6th, After six months of reading this Book, I finally read a verse that I completely understand. It changed my whole life. It's the teaching from Christ when he appeared to America. He taught in 3 Nephi 18:20 that every man should pray to Father in His name, if they have faith that their questions will be answered: "And whatsoever ye shall ask the Father in my name, which is right, believing that ye shall receive, behold it shall be given unto you" (3 Nephi 18:20).

When I read it, I just felt so strong that I should pray and ask. With no hesitation, I got on my knees and started to offer a prayer to God. My prayer was simple I can't simplify any more. I only asked: "If there is a God, please let me know why your church doesn't drink beer, coffee and tea."

Even if just, a prayer like this, Father answered it. As soon as I finished my prayer, I began to feel a mighty power kinda like a wind pierced my heart and my eyes were suddenly filed with tears, I felt something I haven't ever felt before, I felt I was at home, I can see the love of God and everything was just that bright and hopeful to me. But more important, I know He didn't directly answer my question why

How One Young Man Found God and Changed His Life Forever

his church doesn't drink beer, coffee and tea, but he said to me clearly, He is there. He lives!

That night, I talked to my parents, I have to join this church. And I told them I believe this church is true. My parents were very much shocked when they heard it from my mouth and they didn't go to sleep for the whole night, they felt they lost their son because they were both communist.

They thought a young man has never seen this church before but want to be a part of it, either he is crazy or the church is crazy. They were so confused, but I felt nothing can stop me from being baptized. With this sincere desire, I started to read the scriptures with my parents, they said there is no God, but I know Father lives and I know he knows it too. Finally, after three weeks, I got permission from my parents to be baptized. And short after, I faced the biggest challenge during my conversion journey.

I found out the only place I can be baptized was in Hong Kong which if I take train, it will cost me twenty-four hours to get to there. It's in a totally different part of China. But nothing can stop me to be baptized since then. I packed my luggage, left Beijing. At that time, I just turned fifteen. However, since I had never been to a LDS church before I didn't know where I should go in Hong Kong. The only resource I had was a map. I checked to see where is LDS

Church, so I saw the big sign says LDS temple on the map, I thought if I go there I may have a chance to be baptized. So I took all of my bags and headed to temple.

After 30 minutes, two young men came and talked to me about their church. They were so nice to me and introduced themselves as the Mormon missionaries. I told them I want to join the Church. They were so surprised.

So they taught me all of the lessons in one day and I joined the Church that night. My baptism only had three people, however, the spirit was really strong and I felt so clean after I got baptized. Consequently I was confirmed as a member of this church.

After the baptism, I had a chance to go to the LDS Church first time in my life in Hong Kong. I would never forget it, because I finally saw the real LDS members like my friend said to me five years ago, I myself that day, I want to become like them.

Shortly after, I came back to Beijing, became the number seventh member in my whole city, which has 30 million people. On the first Sabbath day in Beijing I couldn't even believe my eyes because I thought the Church in Beijing was so different than the Church in Hong Kong. We met in a small apartment with six people and only had 30 minutes Sacrament, no Sunday school, no third hour, only Sacrament and that's all.

How One Young Man Found God and Changed His Life Forever

However, I didn't give up on going there. I realized no matter what does the Church look like, the gospel is still true and perfect.

Little by little the Church gradually began to grow, from seven members to 50, from 50 members to 150, and after a year I got a chance to baptize my mom who had been to church for over ten months. Recently, she got called to be the Relief Society President. And five years later, we have two branches and more than 400 members over there in Beijing. It's truly a miracle of the Lord. It testifies to us that the Church is true and nothing can stop the gospel moving forward.

Two years ago I left on my mission, I was the third missionary from Beijing, but two years later, we have 15 missionaries right now who are serving outside from Beijing, ten more are preparing the sleeves to serve. The Church in China was really growing! And certainly it's still growing, I believe one day we will see a holy temple called Beijing, China on that place.

Elder Guo's testimony touched my heart and brought tears to my eyes when I first read it, especially the part where he tells us he had never even heard the name of Christ before his friend told him about God. His story tears me up each time I read it or share it with others. Let us plead with the Lord that the spiritual darkness that now covers China and other parts of the world will be lifted and that the light of Christ will filter down to the earth more abundantly throughout the earth.

If we will all unite with our faith and prayers and fasting we can accomplish something wonderful! I make this promise by virtue of the faith I have in Christ. If we will all believe and unite in fasting and prayer in behalf of the Chinese people, we will see one million new members of the Church in China twenty years after our full-time missionaries arrive there. There will also be a temple of the Lord in Beijing, China at that time.

Update on Elder Guo:

Elder Guo has returned to Bejing, China having completed his two-year mission in America. One of the first things he was able to do upon his return was to baptize his father. He has now had the privilege of baptizing both of his parents.

Chapter Three

Are You Spiritually Dead?

Not long ago I discovered a fun and easy way to test ourselves and find out if our spiritual engines are alive and filled with power or if they might need a minor or a complete tune-up or even a complete overhaul!

Please remember, Christ can change your heart and give you a new heart. He who made your heart from the dust of the earth certainly has the power to change your heart and make your heart brand new and allow you to have a mighty change of heart.

Music has always held a special place in my life. On any given day there will be a song playing in my head. I have always appreciated a well-written song. Not just any song can qualify. The lyrics must be clever, inventive and unique not just original. The chorus must be inviting and fun to listen to. There must be a hook that pulls you in and immediately makes you want to hear the song again and again. When all of these elements work, you have a well-written song.

Most well written songs become classics. But in order to live and to take on a life of their own even the best songs need an extraordinary arrangement and they must be performed by a singer who can project not just feeling but raw, unabashed emotion into the song and let the song literally be born and have its own life.

Once in a while, a singer will emerge who has the ability to not merely take us to heaven by singing a song but to bring a little bit of heaven to us. I offer you the magnificent performances of three songs that will allow you to know there is something more around us than what we can see with our eyes and hear with our ears.

Please listen to these songs with an open heart and an open mind. But I give you fair warning, if you can listen to any one of these songs and not feel there is something greater than man, if you do not have tears come to your eyes and feel your heart and the spirit of God stir within you and even feel the presence of God and angels then I have bad news for you. You are not just spiritually dead; you have probably been dead and buried for more than a month.

Only the precise performances and recordings of these songs by the precise artists listed below will work for this experiment.

Here are the songs:
Nessun Dorma sung by Luciano Pavorotti, live in Central Park, New York, June 28, 1993.
Over the Rainbow, sung by Judy Garland, from the Motion Picture, "The Wizard of Oz" 1939.
I Dreamed a Dream from, "Les Miserables" sung by Susan Boyle, her first audition for Britain's Got Talent, June 24, 2010.

Are you spiritually alive or are you spiritually DEAD? If you are spiritually dead it is time to, awake and arise from the dead. "Awake thou that sleepest, and arise from the dead, and Christ shall give thee light" (Ephesians 5:14).

Chapter Four

How to Recharge Your Spiritual Self

When our car engine is cold it will not pass the emissions test. Sometimes even when a car engine warms up it will still fail the emissions test. Some engines will need either a minor or a complete tune-up to pass. It is the same with our spiritual engine, or the light of Christ, which God has placed within us. Some folks will need a minor or a complete spiritual tune-up. One man told me: "When it comes to this religion stuff, I'll be needin' a complete overhaul." I said, "Over all, overhaul is good. Don't forget to wear overalls." He smiled at that.

The smallest act of kindness will cause

the light of Christ that is in you to grow brighter. But the smallest act of selfishness will cause the light in you, to grow a little more dim. The gospel of Jesus Christ teaches us to be unselfish. Jesus teaches us to love. God is love. Love is of God. Everyone who loves is of God but he that hates his brother is not of God and the light of Christ that was once in the man who hates his neighbor will have diminished. Should any man continue to hate his neighbor and be selfish and prideful that man will eventually be filled with darkness and there will be no more light left, in him.

If you want to get more of the light of Christ inside of yourself then spend some time losing yourself in the scriptures. By scriptures I mean, "The King James" translation of the Bible and "The Book of Mormon." If you would like a free copy of the "King James" translation of the Bible or the Book of Mormon or both, just call these toll free numbers:

(888) 537-7700 within the United States.
(or) 1-(888) 537-7700 when outside of the United States.

When your scriptures arrive, begin reading the Book of Mormon. I love all of the scriptures God has given to us in these latter days. But God has attached a special promise to those who will read the Book of Mormon. I have seen hundreds of people take God at his word when it comes to the following promise and they have all been baptized.

This is the promise pertaining to reading the Book of Mormon, "And when ye shall receive these things, I would exhort you that ye would ask God, the Eternal Father, in the name of Christ, if these things are not true; and if ye shall ask with a sincere heart having faith in Christ, he will manifest the truth of it unto you, by the power of the Holy Ghost. And by the power of the Holy Ghost, ye may know the truth of all things" (Moroni 10:4-5).

Just this one verse from the Bible was enough to motivate young Joseph Smith to pray and ask God which of all the churches he should join: "If any of you lack wisdom, let him ask of God that giveth to all men liberally, and upbraideth not and it shall be given him" (James 1:5).

One verse from the Book of Mormon was enough to cause Elder Guo to pray and find God and join the Church of Jesus Christ of Latter-day Saints and to then become a full-time missionary: "And whatsoever ye shall ask the Father in my name, which is right, believing that ye shall receive, behold it shall be given unto you" (3 Nephi 18:20).

How to Recharge Your Spiritual Self

Reading the scriptures daily will not fail to keep your spiritual engine alive and working and filled with light. Get in the habit of reading the scriptures daily and then pondering what you have read. Learn to ask good and specific questions when you pray and God will then be able to give you specific answers to your prayers.

What does one have to do to get more of the light of Christ? Answer: Read the Book of Mormon daily and then pray and ask God if it is true. Do many small acts of kindness.

That is all you have to do to get more of the light of Christ inside of you. Now you will be able to see more clearly to, change your life for the better forever.

Chapter Five

The Light of Christ

One of the greatest gifts our beloved Father in heaven has given man is the ability to feel things deeply. When a man can do this, that man can love. The light of Christ allows, permits and enables all men to love because the light of Christ comes from Jesus Christ and that light is in all men who come into the world.

Jesus said, "By this shall all men know that ye are my disciples, if ye have love one to another" (John 13:35). John the Beloved continued to explain: "If we walk in the light, as he is in the light, we have fellowship one with another, and the blood of Jesus Christ his Son cleanseth us from all sin" (1 John 1:7).

The Light of Christ

It is the duty of all men to love everything God's hands have made. The light of Christ enables all men to do that. A certain Pharisee who was a lawyer once asked Jesus a question tempting him. Said he, "Master which is the great commandment in the law" (Matthew 22: 36)? Jesus said unto him, "Thou shalt love the Lord thy God with all thy heart and with all thy soul and with all thy mind. This is the first great commandment. And the second is like unto it, thou shalt love thy neighbor as thyself" (Matthew 22:37-39). No man can do that without the light of Christ, therefore, we will want to get as much of the Savior's light in us as we possibly can. Certainly one of the most descriptive name titles of Jesus Christ is: "I am the light of the world" (John 8:12). Jesus Christ "is that true light which lighteth every man that cometh into the world" (John 1:9).

Every man woman and child born on this earth was given two things from God in addition to their physical bodies when they were born. All men, women and children were given a portion of the light of Christ and all were given their agency from God. Therefore, we all have a part of God in us. The light of Christ that is in us allows us to love everything God's hands have made. And he has made everything. The light of Christ also allows man to know the difference between good and evil. Agency allows all men the privilege to choose to either follow the good and the light or to follow the evil and darkness. Agency allows all of mankind to govern themselves: to choose for themselves. God never intended any man to be ruled or dominated by another man. God is not the author of slavery and dictatorships. From the God inspired, "Declaration of Independence" the founding fathers of America have left us these immortal words, "We hold these truths to be self-evident, that all men are created equal, that they are endowed by their Creator with certain unalienable Rights, that among these are Life, Liberty and the pursuit of Happiness" (From the Declaration of Independence, In Congress, July 4, 1776).

    Jesus taught in his Sermon on the Mount, (speaking of his Father) "he maketh his sun to rise on the evil and on the good, and sendeth rain of the just and on the unjust" (Matthew 5:45). The light of Christ once again, allows man to love. Love is of God. Hatred is of the devil and is darkness. John the Beloved taught us: "He that saith he is in the light, and hateth his brother, is in darkness even until now. He that loveth his brother abideth in the light, and there is none occasion of stumbling in him. But he that hateth his brother is in darkness and walketh in darkness, and knoweth not whiter he goeth, because that darkness hath blinded his eyes" (John 1:9-11). John continued to instruct us

The Light of Christ

with these words, "Beloved let us love one another; for love is of God: and every one that loveth is born of God, and knoweth God. He that loveth not knoweth not God; for God is love" (John 4:7-8).

A portion of the light of Christ is in all of us, therefore let us nurture that light that it might grow brighter and brighter. How do we do that? Once more, the answer is: By learning to love all things God's hands have made. If you are alive, you have a portion of the light of Christ in you. Jesus Christ is the source of the light that is in all men. Jesus is the "true Light which lighteth every man that cometh into the world" (John 1:9). What are you doing with the light that is in you? Is the light of Christ that is in you working? Are you spiritually alive? Perhaps your spiritual engine needs a tune up. Your spiritual engine may need a complete overhaul. Should you suspect that to be the case perhaps one more visit to Chapter Four, may help.

The light of Christ is in every man and is the power thereof and the reason man has light and life and does exist. If a man could look at other men and women with spiritual eyes that man would see that all men have light shining from them just as the stars give off their light at night. Some men would shine more brightly than others because some men have more of the light of Christ in them than others. NASA has recently published photographs of our mother earth taken from the vicinity of Saturn and one can see the earth giving off her light just as the stars in heaven give off their light at night.

The Light of Christ

Change Your Life Forever

The Light of Christ

Jesus has taught us thus: "The light of the body is the eye. If thy eye be single to my glory, thy whole body shall be filled with light. But if thy eye be evil, thy whole body shall be filled with darkness. And if thy body be filled with darkness, how great is that darkness" (Matthew 6:22-23)! Can a man continue to live if his eye is evil and the light that was once in him is now darkness? Apparently yes. There are many evil men and women living in the world. These have denied the Savior and have subjected themselves to the devil. Their bodies are filled with darkness yet they go on living. These go on living because of agency. But for man to begin his life on earth he needs more than the breath of life breathed into his nostrils by God. He needs more than air to breathe, water to drink and food to eat. Man and all living things need the light of Christ to begin life. How much light can a human body hold? Enough until that whole body is filled with light. The Lord's promise to all is: "And if your eye be single to my glory, your whole bodies shall be filled with light, and there shall be no darkness in you; and that body which is filled with light comprehendeth all things" (D&C 88:67).

What a wonderful world it would be if everyone was filled with light and they were able to comprehend all things!

Chapter Six

Man's Origin and Destiny

My neighbor's father sought to understand the answers to the above heading all of his adult life until he met the missionaries who answered all of his questions to his satisfaction.

One Man's Conversion

This is the conversion story of the father of one of my neighbors; Arthur Curtis Wheeler. From his youth my father had questions about who we are, what is God like, why are we here, *and where do we go after death?* Over the years he visited with many men of the clergy, from all faiths. He met with Priests, Rabbis, and various Protestant ministers. None of them could satisfy him with their answers. My mother invited the two missionaries from the Church of Jesus Christ of Latter-day Saints, who had joined the choir in the Congregationalist church where we attended for a Saturday night dinner. She told them she was not interested in their message, but her husband might be. When the missionaries met my father, he told them he had certain questions that had concerned him his whole life, and that the other ministers could not answer his questions. He told the missionaries that if they could answer his questions to his satisfaction, "he was their man." They did and he was baptized shortly after in a YMCA pool. He was faithful and served valiantly until his death at the age of 89. My father served a mission later in life as a seventy.

Man's Origin

Man did not always live on the earth. Before the advent of man on the earth, all of the spirit sons and daughters of God lived with God the Eternal Father in heaven. God the Eternal Father is the father of the spirit bodies of all mankind. God made the spirit bodies of all men and women in heaven before he made physical man to inhabit the earth. We read from the Book of Moses in the Pearl of Great Price, "All things were made spiritually in heaven, before they were naturally upon the earth" (See, Moses 3:5; 7).

When all the spirit sons and daughters of the Father were made in heaven, (Christ being the firstborn spirit offspring of the Father) the earth was then ready to be created. "And then the Lord said: Let us go down. And they went down at the beginning, and they, that is the Gods, organized and formed the heavens and the earth" (Abraham: 4:1). Once the earth was made, the Son of God created "natural or physical man" under the direction of the Father. God breathed the breath of life into father Adam's nostrils and the first man Adam, the father of the human race, became a living soul. (See Moses 3:7). The scripture says "and man became a living soul, the first flesh upon the earth, the first man also" (See, Moses 3:7). Therefore, Adam is the father of all living. God then made a help meet for Adam. Eve also became a living soul and the mother of all living.

God made a garden eastward, in Eden for the man and the woman. When Adam and Eve lived in the Garden of Eden they had terrestrial and immortal bodies. That is, they were made to live forever. The Garden of Eden was a terrestrial place.

There were trees of every kind there, which bore fruit for them to eat and God also planted the tree of life in the garden and the tree of the knowledge of good and evil. Adam and Eve were told that of every tree in the garden they could eat but of the tree of the knowledge of good and evil they could not eat neither should they touch it lest they die. Satan or the devil tempted Eve and she did partake of the tree of the knowledge of good and evil. Because of disobedience, Adam and Eve were cast out of the Garden of Eden into the lone and dreary world. The man Adam and his wife Eve were told that they would die. "And all the days that Adam lived were 930 years: and he died" (Genesis 5:5).

The Spirit World

God also made a place for man to go when he dies. This place is known as the spirit world. The world of spirits is very near the earth. The spirit world is divided into two separate places.

Paradise

Paradise is where the righteous spirits of God go to await their resurrection. "It is a state of happiness, a state of rest, a state of peace, where they shall rest from all their troubles and from all care and sorrow" (Alma 40:11-14). Paradise is literally "heaven" for the righteous spirit sons and daughters of God while they await their resurrection that will come when the Savior returns to the earth.

When the first resurrection begins, "the spirits of the righteous" shall be reunited with their bodies, and in immortal glory "the righteous shall have a perfect knowledge of their enjoyment, and their righteousness, being clothed with purity, yea, even with the robe of righteousness" (2 Nephi 9:13-14). "The prophet Joseph Smith has also said: "When men are prepared, they are better off to go hence. The spirits of the just are exalted to a greater and more glorious work: hence they are blessed in their departure to the world of spirits" (Teachings p. 326).

Spirit Prison

Spirit prison is where the wicked or unrighteous spirits go. Spirit prison is a temporary resting place for the unrighteous. Therefore, when a man dies, his spirit body leaves his physical body and that spirit body either goes to paradise, which is a temporary resting place for the righteous or it goes to spirit prison, which is a place for the unrighteous.

The Judgment

The day will come when all men will stand before God to be judged according to their works. We do not know when that day will be. The Lord has not revealed when he will return to the earth.

The Resurrection

However, because Christ has conquered death through the resurrection, we have the certain promise that all of mankind will be resurrected. Speaking to Martha about her brother Lazarus whom Jesus raised from the dead the Savior of the world said, "I am the resurrection and the life: he that believeth in me, though he were dead, yet shall he live" (John 11:25). I have not yet died and been resurrected but I have a perfect knowledge by the power of the Holy Ghost that all will be resurrected. You can obtain that same knowledge in the same way.

Chapter Seven

The Plan of Salvation

    The Plan of Salvation is God the Eternal Father's plan written by His own hand that shows all of mankind: How To Change For The Better Forever! A careful comparison of the Plan of Salvation and the gospel and doctrine of Jesus Christ will reveal that all three of these; work in harmony and in conjunction with one another. But the plan of salvation was conceived and written by; operates by and comes from, the Father.
    The central part or the heart of the Plan of Salvation is the atonement of Jesus Christ. But even with the atonement of Jesus Christ and the steps of repentance clearly spelled out by the Father, the Plan of Salvation cannot work for man without natural man's active participation in it. The Plan of Salvation can only work for man

when the natural man allows the spirit of God to humble him to the point when he can become meek and lowly and willing to submit to all things, which God can inflict upon him.

"For the natural man is an enemy to God, and has been from the fall of Adam, and will be, forever and ever, unless he yields to the enticings of the Holy Spirit, and putteth off the natural man and becometh a saint through the atonement of Christ the Lord, and becometh as a child, submissive, meek, humble, patient, full of love, willing to submit to all things which the Lord seeth fit to inflict upon him, even as a child doth submit to his father" Mosiah 3:19).

The next time you are corrected by someone and thereby humbled without your invitation to anyone who may put you through that experience, consider this: "He whom the Lord loveth he correcteth; even as a father, the son in whom he delighteth" (Proverbs 3:12). So the next time you experience an uninvited correction just remember, the Lord must love you a lot.

Let us remember that man is here on the earth living in a natural body to be tested. Most men have forgotten living with God in heaven in their spirit bodies. It is the tendency of almost all men living on the earth to be selfish and to think only of themselves and perhaps, to also think of their loved ones. But Christ has given us a higher law:

"Ye have heard that it hath been said, Thou shalt love thy neighbor, and hate thine enemy. But I say unto you, Love your enemies, bless them that curse you, do good to them that despitefully use you, and persecute you: That ye may be the children of your Father which is in heaven: for he maketh his sun to shine on the evil and the good, and sendeth rain on the just and on the unjust" (Matthew 5: 43-45).

The list of things we must do to follow the Father's Plan of Salvation have been clearly spelled out in the scripture: "But God hath made it known unto our fathers that all men must repent. And he called upon our father Adam by his own voice, saying: I am God; I made the world, and men before they were in the flesh" (Moses 6:50-51).

And he also said unto him: "If thou will turn unto me, and hearken unto my voice, and believe, and repent of all thy transgressions, and be baptized even in water, in the name of mine Only Begotten Son, who is full of grace and truth, which is Jesus Christ, the only name which shall be given under heaven unto the children of men, ye shall receive the gift of the Holy Ghost, asking all things in his name, and whatsoever ye shall ask, it shall be given you" (Moses 6:52).

The Plan of Salvation

"And now, behold, I say unto you: This is the plan of salvation unto all men, through the blood of mine Only Begotten, who shall come in the meridian of time"(Moses 6:62). The Plan of Salvation can only work when man follows all the steps spelled out by the Father and by strict obedience to those requirements, endures all things until the end. (See 2 Nephi 31:20).

And when we do these things, it is by and through and because of the atonement of Jesus Christ and the grace of Christ that we are saved.

"For it is by grace that ye are saved after all we can do" (2 Nephi 25:23). The Father is continually reminding man that without Jesus Christ we cannot return to live with him in heaven. The Savior said: " I am the way, the truth, and the life, no man cometh unto the Father, but by me" (John 14:6).

"Wherefore, ye must press forward with a stedfastness in Christ, having a perfect brightness of hope, and a love of God and for all men. Wherefore if ye shall press forward, feasting upon the word of Christ and endure to the end, behold, thus saith the Father: ye shall have eternal life" (2 Nephi 31:20).

True happiness comes from living the Father's Plan of Salvation. Happiness and even joy can come from sharing the Father's Plan of Happiness with the world.

Chapter Eight

The Infinite Atonement

The perfect and infinite atonement of Jesus Christ is the single most important event to happen on this earth in the history of mankind. Without the atonement of Jesus Christ, when men die, their physical bodies would be left to smolder in the dust. There would be no resurrection or reuniting of the spirits of men with their physical bodies without the atonement of Jesus Christ. Therefore, man could not receive a fullness of joy. Men could not return to live with God in heaven again forever but the spirit bodies of all mankind would remain in hell being subject to the devil.

Jesus said of himself: "I came to the world to do the will of my Father to be nailed to the cross to atone for the sins of all men that I might draw all men to me" (3 Nephi 27:13-22).

What is the atonement of Jesus Christ? It

is the redeeming power that gives all of mankind the ability to return to live with the Father and the Son in heaven once again if they will repent and be obedient in keeping all of God's commandments and endure until the end.

I have heard many say, "I am not good enough to go to heaven." None of us is good enough without Jesus Christ. "For all have sinned and come short of the glory of God" (Romans 3:23).

Without experiencing the suffering and agony and pain that Jesus suffered for all of mankind in the Garden of Gethsemane and on the cross at Calvary, it will impossible for any man to ever say he fully understands the height, depth and breadth of the atonement. Only when man separates himself from the natural man can he begin to comprehend the magnificence and grandeur of the atonement.

Because of the atonement of Jesus Christ, when a man sins and breaks one of the commandments of God, he can repent and start again. Without the atonement of Jesus Christ, when men sin, they would have to pay the price for their sins by themselves which is something that mere mortal man could never do.

Jesus Christ is the chosen Savior of the world. Jesus Christ has paid the price for the sins of all men who have ever or will ever live on this world and upon millions of other worlds, worlds without end. The prophet Moses has written "And mine only begotten IS AND SHALL BE THE SAVIOR" (Moses 1:7). Please note that God the Eternal Father has said that Jesus not only shall be the Savior of the world but that Jesus Christ IS the Savior of the world. Therefore, before the earth was formed, before father Adam was born, before Jesus was born, before Christ began his mortal ministry-Jesus Christ already IS the Savior of the world!

    The Savior of the world is Jesus Christ and it is Jesus Christ and no other who has accomplished the atonement of Jesus Christ for all of mankind. The atonement of Jesus Christ is the enabling power that let's all of mankind become worthy (or good enough) if man will love God and keep his commandments. Because Jesus Christ has paid the price for our sins and not for our sins only but for the sins of all who have ever lived on the millions of other worlds God has created, worlds without end. That is why we speak of the atonement as the infinite atonement.

    But we must also endure until the end. The Lord said: "he that shall endure until the end, the same shall be saved" (Matthew 24:13). And how are we ultimately saved? "It is by grace that we are saved, after all we can do" (2 Nephi 25:23).

To all who do this, thus saith the Father: "ye shall have eternal life" (2 Nephi 31:20).

The following story comes from one of my neighbors who is currently serving as our neighborhood bishop: "When I was a young resident at Cook County Hospital in Chicago, I was on call on one busy Saturday night. I was called to the trauma unit to take care of a woman. This woman was a woman of the evening and she had displeased her employer and he had cut her face with a broken bottle. The cut went all across her face. We were too busy that night to have any room in the OR (operating room) so I had to take care of her in the trauma unit using a local anesthetic. I spent a couple of hours taking care of this massive wound across her face. When this woman came in, she was frightened. She was distrustful, she was angry and she was utterly devastated by this wound that she had on her face. But during that couple of hours I was able to reassure her. I was able to calm her down.

Now, I didn't necessarily approve of her life style. I didn't necessarily approve of the circumstances, which brought her into my care. I learned very early in my profession that when I treated patients with respect and with love, they responded in kind. This woman was no exception. During my career I have had the opportunity to treat people from all walks of life imaginable, and some that you could not even imagine. And I have found that when you treat somebody as a child of our Father in heaven, they always respond. I have found that to be universal. In our world today, I see so much contention. There is no civility. There is plain meanness out there. I see this in sports. I see this in business. I see this in politics. Just because you disagree with someone it doesn't mean that you hate them-or that you are demeaning them. But in the same token, if you love somebody deeply, it doesn't mean that you agree with everything they say or do.

I am so grateful for the atonement of Jesus Christ. I know that He lives. I know that this is His church. I know that He performed the atonement for us. Even with my best treatment and the best skill that I have, the woman I treated will always have a scar. But when the Savior heals there is no scar. It is like it never happened. I love Him for this. And He can do this for us all."

I like this story for three reasons: First, it teaches us that we should love all people just as they are, without judging them and second: this story teaches us that although we may love someone deeply that doesn't mean we have to agree with everything they say and do. Most importantly, this story illustrates the difference between the healing power of man and the healing power of the atonement of Jesus Christ.

There are no scars when Jesus heals us.

He who made us can say, "Go and sin no more." I love the story of Jesus and the woman taken in adultery. Jesus said, "Woman, where are those thine accusers? Hath no man condemned thee? She said, No man, Lord. And Jesus said unto her, neither do I condemn thee, go and sin no more" (John 8:10-11). "Go and sin no more." Can you feel the power of those words? He who made our heart can give us a new heart, a changed heart, and we can begin our lives again. On another occasion Jesus said, "thy sins are forgiven thee, and thou shalt be blessed" (Enos verse 5). What manner of man could speak those words with confidence and authority? To my knowledge, no one in recorded history has ever done so. But Jesus is no ordinary man. He is the Savior of the world, our redeemer and our advocate with the Father and I love and honor him for it. Some folks remember the Savior by seeing him nailed to the cross. I think of our beloved Savior as the living Christ who has conquered death and risen to return to his Father in heaven.

On a certain day, Jesus explained to his apostles: "I came forth from the Father and am come into the world: again, I leave the world and go to the Father" (John 16:28). When Jesus finished his mortal ministry the scriptural account records: "And when he had spoken these things, while they beheld, he was taken up; and a cloud received him out of their sight. And while they looked stedfastly toward heaven as he went up, behold, two men stood by them in white apparel; Which also said, Ye men of Galilee, why stand ye gazing up into heaven? This same Jesus, which is taken up from you into heaven, shall so come in like manner as ye have seen him go into heaven" (Acts 1: 9-11).

Chapter Nine

Grace

    The Grace of Jesus Christ is the enabling power that allows all of mankind to return to heaven to live with the Father and the Son again forever. In mortality, Jesus grew from grace to grace. We have the testimony of John: "And I, John, bear record that I beheld his glory, as the glory of the Only Begotten of the Father, full of grace and truth, even the Spirit of truth, which came and dwelt in the flesh and dwelt among us. And I, John, saw that he received not of the fullness at the first, but received grace for grace; And he received not of the fullness at first but continued from grace to grace, until he received a fullness; And thus he was called the Son of God, because he received not of the fullness at the first" (D&C 93: 11-14).
    If one has grace he has the capacity to possess great amounts of: compassion, kindness,

mercy, and charity for his fellow man, even to the laying down of his life for a friend. Grace is an attribute of perfection possessed by Deity. God teaches us throughout the scriptures that man must grow from grace to grace even as the Son of God grew from grace to grace. It is clear that more and more of the light of Christ is required to learn more and more of spiritual things and for man to obtain more and more grace and truth and that a fullness of light and truth comes one little sliver of light and truth at a time. "And if your eye be single to my glory, your whole body shall be filled with light, and there shall be no darkness in you; and that body which is filled with light comprehendeth all things" (D&C 88:67). And it follows that a body that is filled with light will also be filled with grace and truth since the promise is, that body, *"comprehendeth all things" (D&C 88:67).*

The Lord has told us how to make this happen, "Therefore, sanctify yourselves that your minds become single to God, and the days will come that you shall see him; for he will unveil his face unto you, and it shall be in his own time, and in his own way, and according to his own will" (D&C 88:68).

Chapter Ten

What Think Ye of Christ?

Some time ago I had an unusual dream. In my dream there were six college-aged young men and women standing on a stage and facing me. They were dressed in their Sunday best. There was a podium on the stage. On the front of the podium there was a cross. The cross was shining as if it were a neon sign.

There was something about those young people that stood out to me right away. There was no spirit of love about them. They projected an air of superiority.

One of the young men moved behind the podium as if he were about to speak. In my dream I was still standing. I moved closer to the podium about 20 feet away. I asked them, "What think ye of Christ" (Matthew 22:42)? (See also, Matthew 16:16; John 11:27).

What happened next left an indelible impression on my mind. All six of these young men and women who were still standing turned their backs to me. They just stood there with their backs facing me, without saying a word. Then the dream faded away.

Jesus spoke about a certain people during his mortal ministry. Said he: "This people draweth nigh unto me with their mouth, and honoreth me with their lips, but their heart is far from me" (Matthew 15:8). The young people in my dream did not bother to honor Christ with their lips, they turned their backs on me and they turned their backs on Christ without uttering a single word!

When Jesus asked the apostle Peter, "what think ye of Christ?" Peter answered, "thou art the Christ, the Son of the living God" And Jesus answered him, "blessed art thou Simon Barjona for flesh and blood hath not revealed it unto thee, but my Father which is in Heaven and upon this rock (the rock of revelation) I will build my church; and the gates of hell shall not prevail against it" (Matthew 16:17-18; emphasis added).

"No man can say Jesus is Lord but by the Holy Ghost" (1Corinthians 12:3). "No man can receive the Holy Ghost without receiving revelations. The Holy Ghost is a revelator" (Teachings of the Prophet Joseph Smith, see, Joseph Fielding Smith (1976), page 328).

This is what we all need. We need the gift and power of the Holy Ghost to reveal to each of us that Jesus is the Christ, the Son of the living God.

The day will come when every one will have to answer the question, "What think ye of Christ" for themselves. The day will come when every knee shall bow and every tongue confess that Jesus is the Christ and that his is the only name given under heaven whereby men may be saved. (See Acts 4:12).

How will you answer? What will your answer be? What think ye of Christ?

Chapter Eleven

Will Christ Still Rescue the Sinner?

Jesus came into the world not to condemn the world of sin but to save the world from sin" (See, John 3:17).

Christ will take you as you are and wherever you are and change your heart and give you a new heart *IF* you will but hear his voice and then open the door and let him in. Jesus said, "Behold, I stand at the door and knock, if any man shall hear my voice and open the door, I will come in and sup with him, and he with me" (Revelation 1:20).

It doesn't make any difference what you have done; Christ has paid the price for your sins. "Though your sins be as scarlet, they shall be white as snow" (Isaiah 1:18). Christ has paid the price for all of your sins, not just for little sins but for big ones too. Not just for the sins of some but for the sins of every man woman and child who ever lived. Will you take advantage of his atonement or will you ignore what the Savior of the world has done for you? Only Christ can forgive sins and Christ only can change your heart and give you a new heart and that by the power of his perfect and infinite atonement. There is one unpardonable sin.

The Prophet Joseph Smith explained, "No man can commit the unpardonable sin after the dissolution of the body, nor in this life, until he receives the Holy Ghost" (TPJS, p. 357). To commit the unpardonable sin, a person "must receive the Holy Ghost, have the heavens opened unto him, and know God, and then sin against Him. After a man has sinned against the Holy Ghost, there is no repentance for him... he has got to deny Jesus Christ when the heavens have been opened to him, and to deny the Plan of Salvation with his eyes open to the truth of it" (TPJS, p. 358; cf. Heb. 10:26-29)

I know God loves you. God created you. God cares about you. God knows you by your name. God made you with his own hands from the dust of the earth and God breathed the breath of life into your nostrils and you became a living soul. God also put the light of Christ in you that you might be always able to tell the difference between good and evil and that you might be able to see the things of God, while you are alive and living.

Test to Know Good from Evil

This is how you may know the difference between good and evil: "For behold the Spirit of Christ is given to every man, that he may know good from evil; wherefore, I show unto you the way to judge; for every thing which inviteth to do good, and to persuade to believe in Christ is sent forth by the power and gift of Christ; wherefore ye may know with a perfect knowledge it is from God" (Moroni 7:16).

"But whatsoever thing persuadeth men to do evil, and believe not in Christ, and deny him, and serve not God, then ye may know with a perfect knowledge it is of the devil; for after this manner doth the devil work, for he persuadeth no man to do good no, not one; neither do his angels; neither do they who subject themselves unto him" (Moroni 7:17).

This is the test to use to know the difference between good and evil and not just to know: but to know with a perfect knowledge. So, fear not, all these things are true. Jesus has promised, "Let not your heart be troubled: ye believe in God, believe also in me. In my Father's

Will Christ Still Rescue the Sinner?

house are many mansions: if were not so, I would have told you. I go to prepare a place for you. And if I go and prepare a place for you, I will come again and receive you unto myself; that where I am, there you may be also" (John 14:1-3).

Chapter Twelve

Has the Day of Miracles Ceased?

    I grew up with a story my mother told me about her brother Herbert. When he was a young boy, Herbert climbed up to the top of one of the steel towers that held electrical lines. While climbing he somehow managed to touch the electrical wires and he was electrocuted. When he was brought home, he was placed on the kitchen table in my grandmother's home. Following the attempt to save his life, he was pronounced dead. My grandmother would not accept that and so she prayed with faith in Christ that her son would live. Her son did come alive again. That was a miracle and that story became the foundation of my faith in Christ as a young boy. I can still remember going to my grandmother's home as a young boy. When I walked into her home, there was a painting of Jesus praying in the Garden of Gethsemane placed on the wall just before you entered her living room. I'm certain I did not understand what that painting meant to my grandmother back then, but I do now.

I was able to visit more than one hospital while I was serving in Cam Rahn Bay, Viet Nam and on one occasion I stopped to talk with a young soldier who had been hit with an AK-47 round. The bullet entered his left wrist and went all the way up his arm and exited out of his left shoulder. Had the bullet continued and entered his neck, he would not have survived.

While serving in Da Nang it came my turn to pull guard duty. It was monsoon season and there was lots of water and mud everywhere. I was assigned to pull guard duty in a guard tower from sun down to sun up with only one break during the night. The very next day we would all get to see the Bob Hope show and of course, that was something everyone was looking forward to.

Two rockets landed in the mud that night. They came in from another direction away from my guard tower. Had those two rockets exploded who knows how many men would have died including myself? Now for one rocket not to explode is one thing. But for two rockets to land, even in the mud and not explode is a miracle.

    I know what it is like to have a rocket explode near you. When I was in Cam Rahn Bay, Viet Nam a rocket did come in while I was at the Air Force Check in and out gate with our local Vietnamese workers. I was driving them back to their village in an Army pick-up truck. I was the only military person in the truck. I had no weapon. Anyone could easily hear the rocket coming in from more than 100 yards away. You should have seen how fast the Vietnamese workers who were in the pick-up truck scrambled for safety under the truck! The rocket exploded about 100 yards away on part of an Air Force runway. The fact that that rocket did not land near enough to us to injure any of us is also a miracle.

    Several years ago, I was on a business trip driving from Ft. Collins to Denver, Colorado on a snowy winter day. The highway had black ice on it but I didn't know that until I ran over some of it while driving down a long low grade. To make matters worse, two semi trucks were coming up the mountain on the other side of the highway. When I hit black ice I had no control of steering. The car was in a spin and out of control. I was headed right for the two semi trucks coming up the mountain. I did the only thing I knew would work, I prayed. I prayed with the faith I had in Christ and the car broke free of the black ice and the tires found solid road just in time to get enough traction to steer my way to safety. That was a miracle and I thank God for it.

Jesus Christ has made a promise to all: "Whatsoever thing ye shall ask the Father in my name, which is good, in faith believing that ye shall receive, behold, it shall be done unto you" (Moroni 7: 27). I did ask with faith in Christ. My grandmother did ask with faith in Christ and we were both granted that which we prayed for in faith.

I think we may all tend to take miracles for granted too often. When we grow older however, and have had time to reflect on how many times we could have died; the hand of God in our lives becomes a whole lot easier to see. Miracles become more real to us and we realize the day of miracles has not ceased.

The time to develop faith in Christ is not when your car is spinning out of control on black ice headed for two semi trucks. If that ever happens to you, you will have 10 or perhaps 20 seconds until you crash and die. The time to develop faith in Christ is long before anything like that happens to you. Then when a life-threatening situation occurs, you will have confidence God will answer your prayer because of your faith in Christ.

John the Beloved has told us how to have confidence in God, "For if our heart condemn us, God is greater than our heart, and knoweth all things. Beloved, if our heart condemn us not, then have we confidence toward God. And whatsoever we ask, we receive of him, because we keep his commandments, and do those things that are pleasing in his sight. And this is the commandment, that we should believe on the name of his Son Jesus Christ, and love one another, as he gave us commandment. And he that keepeth his commandments dwelleth in him, and he in him. And hereby we know that he abideth in us, by the Spirit which he hath given us" (1 John 3:20-22).

Chapter Thirteen

Who Is God?

    "The heavens declare the glory of God and the firmament showeth his handiwork" (Psalms 19:1). Indeed, if you will look up into the sky on any dark night far from the city lights, you will see God moving in his majesty and glory. When we speak of God, we are generally referring to the Father. The scriptures instruct us that, 'This is life eternal that they might know thee, the only true God, and Jesus Christ whom thou hast sent.' (John 17:3).

The prophet Joseph Smith declared, "If any man does not know God, and inquires what kind of a being He is—if he will search diligently his own heart—if the declaration of Jesus and the apostles be true, he will realize that he has not eternal life; for there can be eternal life on no other principle.

Joseph Smith inquired after the character of God. Said he, "My first object is to find out the character of the only wise and true God, and what kind of a being He is. ...

God Himself was once as we are now, and is an exalted man, and sits enthroned in yonder heavens! That is the great secret. If the veil were rent today, and the great God who holds this world in its orbit, and who upholds all worlds and all things by His power, was to make Himself visible—I say, if you were to see Him today, you would see Him like a man in form—like yourselves in all the person, image, and very form as a man; for Adam was created in the very fashion, image and likeness of God, and received instruction from, and walked, talked and conversed with Him, as one man talks and communes with another.

When we understand the character of God, and know how to come to Him, He begins to unfold the heavens to us, and to tell us all about it. When we are ready to come to Him, He is ready to come to us" (*History of the Church,* 6:303–5, 308).

Who Is God?

Joseph Smith continued, "Having a knowledge of God, we begin to know how to approach Him, and how to ask so as to receive an answer"

The Savior has instructed us how to pray. Jesus taught, "After this manner therefore pray ye: "Our Father which art in heaven, hallowed be thy name" (Matthew 6:9). Next, we thank God, the Eternal Father for the blessings of life. We then ask the Father for that which we may be in need of. Finally, we then close our prayer, in the name of Jesus Christ. Amen.

Three separate and distinct personages make up the Godhead. "We believe in God, the Eternal Father, and in His Son, Jesus Christ, and in the Holy Ghost" (Articles of Faith 1:1).

From the Doctrine and Covenants we read, "The Father has a body of flesh and bones as tangible as man's; the Son also; but the Holy Ghost has not a body of flesh and bones, but is a personage of Spirit. Were it not so, the Holy Ghost could not dwell in us" (D&C 130:22-23).

There are three Gods, The Father, the Son and the Holy Ghost. They are separate and individual personages but they are one in purpose and that purpose is: "to bring to pass the immortality and eternal life of man" (Moses 1:39). The Father and the Son and the Holy Ghost were all present at the baptism of Jesus Christ, showing us that they are indeed, separate and distinct personages. (See, Matthew 3:13-17). "The idea that the Father and the Son dwell in a man's heart is an old sectarian notion, and is false" (D&C 130:3). These three make up the Godhead or the supreme presidency of the Gods of the universe.

God the Father; is the literal father of the spirit body of Jesus Christ who was the firstborn spirit offspring of the Father. We are all spirit sons and daughters of God and Christ is our elder brother. All men who now live on the earth once lived with God the Father in heaven in their spirit bodies. Jesus looks like his father and all of mankind are made in the image and likeness of God. When Phillip asked the Savior: "Shew us the father and it sufficeth us." Jesus replied: "He that hath seen me hath seen the Father" (John 14:9).

Why have we forgotten living with our Father in heaven? Because Satan who is the devil has placed a veil over all the earth and holds that veil in place with a giant chain so that mankind cannot see or remember living with God in heaven. The prophet Enoch beheld Satan in vision and he has left us this record in the Book of Moses within the Pearl of Great Price: "And he (Enoch) beheld Satan, and he had a great chain in his hand, and it veiled the whole face of the earth with darkness; and he looked up and laughed, and his angels rejoiced" (Moses 7:26; emphasis added). It is important to remember that if men could look up into the heavens and see God, how could men develop faith in Him?

Referring to God the Eternal Father, the prophet Joseph Smith explained, "God is the only supreme governor and independent Being in whom all fullness and perfection dwell; who is omnipotent, omnipresent, and omniscient; without beginning of days or end of life; and that in him every good gift and every good principle dwell; and that he is the Father of lights; in him the principle of faith dwells independently, and he is the object in whom the faith of all other rational and accountable beings centers for life and salvation" (Lectures on Faith p. 9).

Chapter Fourteen

Jesus Christ

Jesus Christ is the firstborn spirit Son of God the Eternal Father. Jesus was born of the virgin Mary but Jesus Christ is the Only Begotten Son of God the Eternal Father.

Jesus Christ is the promised Savior. From the time in the pre-existence when the Father called forth his grand council and presented his Plan of Salvation (see Chapter Seven) Jesus Christ forever is, and forever will be, the promised Savior of the world. Speaking to the prophet Moses God said: "and thou art in the similitude of mine Only Begotten; *and mine Only Begotten is and shall be the Savior, for he is full of grace and truth" (Moses 1:6).*

Jesus Christ was chosen by his Father to be the Savior of the world before this world was: "But behold my Beloved Son, which was my Beloved and Chosen from the beginning, said unto me-Father, thy will be done, and the glory be thine forever" (Moses 4:2).

John the Beloved has explained: "For the law was given by Moses but grace and truth came by Jesus Christ" (John 1:17). Jesus Christ is the only name given under heaven whereby men may be saved. (Acts 4:10-12).

Jesus was God in the pre-existence. Jesus prayed to his Father, "And now, O Father, glorify thou me with thine own self with the glory which I had with thee before this world was" (John 17:5). Once again, Jesus was God before the foundation of the world we now live in and he is God now. He is not waiting to become God.

"In the beginning was the word, and the word was with God, and the word was God. The same was in the beginning with God" (John 1:1-2).

Jesus told his disciples who he was and from whence he came. Said he, "I came forth from the Father and am come into the world: again I leave the world, and go to the Father" (John 16:28). With words of humility and reverence for his Father the Son of God spoke, "I can of mine own self do nothing: As I hear, I judge: and my judgment is just because I seek not mine own will, but the will of the Father which hath sent me" (John 5:30).

Jesus Christ, through the direction of his Father, is the creator of all things. "All things were made by him and without him was not anything made that was made" (John 1:3).

Only Jesus Christ can forgive sins. Jesus once asked, "Which is easier to forgive sins or to say, rise up and walk? But that thou might know that I am the Christ I say, "rise up and walk, thy sins are forgiven thee" (Luke 5:23).

To Enos Jesus said, "thy sins are forgiven thee. And there came a voice unto me, saying: Enos, thy sins are forgiven thee, and thou shalt be blessed. And I, Enos knew that God could not lie; wherefore my guilt was swept away" (Enos: verses 5-6).

Jesus Christ is the resurrection and the life. Jesus said to Martha: "I am the resurrection and the life: he that believeth in me, though he were dead, yet shall he live: and whosoever liveth and believeth in me, shall never die. Believest thou this" (John 11: 25-26)? Jesus Christ has conquered death and hell. Because of Jesus Christ all men will be resurrected. The resurrection is a free gift to all of mankind. But eternal life must be earned by obedience to God's commandments and enduring until the end, then we are saved by the grace of God after all we can do.

Jesus Christ Is the Embodiment of Light and Truth

Jesus Christ is the answer to everything pertaining to spiritual light and truth. Christ holds the truth of all things in his hands. Christ is omniscient. That is, Jesus Christ knows all things.

The Savior bore witness of who he is in a modern day revelation: "The Spirit of truth is of God. I am the Spirit of truth, and John bore record of me, saying: He received a fullness of truth, yea, even all truth" (D&C 93: 26). With Christ in a man's life, all men can do whatever is necessary in order to return to live with God and Christ in heaven forever. But without Christ in one's life, all men stumble because of the spiritual darkness, which fills the earth. The apostle Paul understood this principle. Paul has written: "I can do all things through Christ which strengtheneth me" (Philippians 4:13). Jesus said: "I am the true light that lighteth every man that cometh into the world" (D&C 93:2).

Some will tell you that they have power to

take you back to God but that is a lie. Only Jesus Christ can lead all of mankind back to the Father. The Lord has cautioned us, "No man cometh unto the Father but by me" (John 14:6). Jesus declared, "I am the way, the truth and the light" (John 14:6).

Jesus Christ Made Everything

Standing next to his Father in the pre-existence, Jesus Christ made everything. Jesus stretched out the heavens and organized the galaxies and gave order and laws to all things in the universe. (D&C 88:43-44). Jesus Christ made the earth and the moon and our sun and all the stars in the heavens. From the first verse of scripture in the King James translation of the Bible we read: "In the beginning God created the heavens and the earth" (Genesis 1:1). Under the direction of the Father, Jesus made man in his own image, from the dust of the earth, and breathed the breath of life into his nostrils and man became a living soul. (Moses 2:26; Moses 3:7).

John the Beloved said of Jesus Christ, "All things were made by him, and without him was not anything made that was made" (John 1:2). Jesus Christ is the creator of all things. Everything that does exist-was made by him. Paul bore testimony of the true identity of Christ to the Hebrews. The apostle Paul said, "God who at sundry times and in divers manners spake in time past by the prophets, Hath in these last days spoken unto us by his Son, whom he hath appointed heir of all things, by whom also he made the worlds" (Hebrews1:1-2).

"And Thou, Lord, in the beginning hast laid the foundation of the earth; and the heavens are the works of thy hands" (Hebrews 1:10).

Jesus Christ Is God

From the moment, he became the firstborn spirit son of the Father; Jesus Christ is God. He is not waiting to become God as some teach.

Jesus prayed to his Father before his ultimate sacrifice, "And now, O Father, glorify thou me with thine own self with the glory which I had with thee before the world was" (John 16:5).

John the Beloved bore testimony of the Savior with these words, "In the beginning was the Word, and Word was with God, and the Word was God. The same was in the beginning with God" (John 1:1-2).

The apostle Paul helps us to understand the fact that Jesus is God. Speaking of Christ Paul taught, "Who being the brightness of his glory (that is the Father's glory) and the express image of his person, and upholding all things by the word of his power, when he had by himself purged our sins, sat down on the right hand of the majesty on high; Being made so much better than the angels, as he hath by inheritance obtained a more excellent name than they: For unto which of the angels saith he at any time, Thou art my Son, this day have I begotten thee? And again, I will be to him a Father, and he shall be unto me a Son. And again, when he bringeth in the firstbegotten into the world, he saith, And let all the angels of God worship him. And of the angels he saith, Who maketh his angels spirits, and his ministers a flame of fire. *But unto the Son he saith, Thy throne, O God, is forever and ever: a sceptre of righteousness is the sceptre of thy kingdom.* Thou has loved righteousness, and hated iniquity; therefore God, even thy God, hath anointed thee with the oil of gladness above thy fellows" (Hebrews 1: 3-9, emphasis added).

Jesus Christ Is the Savior

With Christ there is no was, but only is. This testimony of the true identity of Jesus Christ is found in the Book of Moses within the Pearl of Great Price, "And I have a work for thee Moses, my son; and thou art in the similitude of mine Only Begotten; *and mine Only Begotten is and shall be the Savior, for he is full of grace and truth"* (Moses 1:6).

From the moment Jesus Christ became the firstborn spirit Son of God the Eternal Father, Jesus is, and shall be, the Savior of the world. We read, "But, behold, my Beloved Son, which was my Beloved and Chosen from the beginning said unto me-Father, thy will be done, and the glory be thine forever" (Moses 4:3). Jesus Christ is the promised Savior. There is no other name given under heaven whereby men may be saved. The prophet Isaiah has given us this testimony of the Son of God, "I, even I, am the Lord, and beside me there is no savior" (Isaiah 43:11). The day will come when every knee shall bow and every tongue shall confess that Jesus is the Christ.

Jesus Christ and His Father Are Gods of Glory

When he saw the Father and the Son, the prophet Joseph Smith said, "I saw two personages whose brightness and glory defy all description" (Joseph Smith 2 17). Moses described God as a "consuming fire" (Deut. 4:24), "his glory consuming everything corrupt and unholy" (D&C 63:34; 101:23-24).

Jesus Is Our Redeemer

What does the word redeem mean? Speaking as a natural man, to redeem is to buy or pay off as in the mortgage of a home. But speaking spiritually, to redeem means to rescue all men, (for all have sinned) from the fall of Adam. Man could not redeem himself; a Savior was required. The Father chose his Only Begotten Son, Jesus Christ to pay the price for the redemption of all mankind by offering himself a ransom for the sins of all, the world. The infinite atonement of Jesus Christ was the price the Savior paid for all of us. Atoning for the sins of the world required the Son of God to voluntarily lay down his life, thus paying the price for the sins of mankind. No one else could do this. "And under no other name doth salvation come" (Acts 4:12).

The apostle Peter declared, "Be it known unto you all, and to all the people of Israel, that by the name of Jesus Christ of Nazareth, whom ye crucified, whom God raised from the dead, even by him doth this man stand before you whole. Neither is there salvation in any other: for there is none other name under heaven given among men, whereby we must be saved" (Acts 4:10,12).

Once again, Jesus Christ is our Redeemer. Christ has atoned for the sins of all those who have or ever will live on this earth and not this earth only but millions of other worlds, worlds without end. When I think of the Savior as our Redeemer I begin to hear the hymn, "Oh Divine Redeemer" in my mind. The people who wrote that hymn knew the true identity of Jesus.

Salvation

Salvation can be thought of as the end result or the blessing that comes from redemption. Thus, once Jesus paid the price for the sins of mankind by and through his infinite atonement, all of mankind could now be saved in the kingdom of God on the conditions of repentance, being baptized, receiving the gift of the Holy Ghost and keeping all of God's commandments and enduring until the end.

Jesus Is Our Advocate with the Father

We have an advocate who pleads our case before the Father. (1 John 2:1).

Jesus Is Our Exemplar

Jesus spent his life on earth doing good works. He healed the sick, lifted up the downhearted, cast out devils, raised the dead, gave hope to the hopeless, forgave sins and spent his days ministering to the needs of others. He is the only man to walk this earth without sin. His perfect example for all of mankind was manifested by him giving the supernal gift to all by laying down his life and atoning for the sins of all, the world. A more perfect example of one's life cannot be found throughout the annals of time.

The very essence of the life of the Savior of the world is found in one word, and that is, "love." I believe it is impossible to love God without loving our neighbors. Conversely, I believe it is impossible for a man to love his neighbor and not to love God. If men could even begin to comprehend the love that God has for them, they would fall down on their knees and give thanks to the God of heaven for all the blessings of life. Let us all give thanks to God for the very air we breathe, for this wonderful planet upon which we dwell, for the gifts and talents we possess and for all of the hidden blessings that are ours.

There is perhaps one scripture from the

Sermon on the Mount that personifies the love our beloved Savior has for all of us. Jesus said, "Ye have heard that it hath been said, Thou shalt love thy neighbor, and hate thine enemy. But I say unto you, Love your enemies, bless them that curse you, do good to them that hate you, and pray for them which despitefully use you, and persecute you. That ye may be the children of your Father which is in heaven: for he maketh his sun to rise on the evil and on the good, and sendeth rain on the just and on the unjust. For if ye love them which love you, what reward have ye? Do not even the publicans, the same? And if ye salute your brethren only, what do ye more than others? Do not even the publican so? Be ye therefore perfect, even as your Father which is in heaven is perfect" (Matthew 5:43-48).

These are words that did not originate with any mortal man. These words alone are proof to me that Jesus came forth from the Father and that he is the promised Savior of the world.

In the Father's supernal wisdom, he has given his beloved Son these words to tell us the way to return to live with him once again. Jesus said, "I am the way, the truth, and the life*: **no man cometh unto the Father but by me**"* (John 14:6, emphasis added).

Chapter Fifteen

The Holy Ghost

The Holy Ghost is a spirit personage in the form of a man. The Holy Ghost has not a body of flesh and bones but is a personage of spirit" (D&C 130: 22). Nephi learned that the Holy Ghost is in the form of a man when he saw him. (1 Nephi 11:11). The Holy Ghost is the third member of the Godhead. Parley P. Pratt described the Holy Ghost with these words: "He is an intelligent being, in the image of God, possessing every organ, attribute, sense, sympathy, and affection that is possessed by God Himself" (Key to Science of Theology, pp.101-1-3). The Prophet Joseph Smith taught us: "The Holy Ghost is a revelator, no man can receive the Holy Ghost without receiving revelations"

The Holy Ghost

(Teachings of the Presidents of the Church: Joseph Smith, 2007, 132).

He is a testator. "No man can say that Jesus is the Lord but by the Holy Ghost" (1Cor. 12:3). He is the Comforter. He brings comfort, peace and assurance to all of mankind.

The Holy Ghost is but one spirit personage. He can only be in one place at one time. But his power and influence fill the immensity of space and thus, the Holy Ghost is omnipresent, like the Father and the Son. The Holy Ghost also shares the same mind and purpose of the Father and the Son, which is: "To bring to pass the immortality and eternal life of man" (Moses 1:39). The Holy Ghost also shares the trait of omniscience with the Father and the Son. The Holy Ghost possesses a fullness of all light and truth. He is the revealer of all truth. "And by the power of the Holy Ghost, ye may know the truth of all things" (Moroni 10:5). Jesus taught: "But the Comforter, which is the Holy Ghost, whom the Father will send in my name, he shall teach you all things and bring all things to your remembrance, whatsoever I have said unto you" John 14:26). I love this scripture because it teaches us that we lived with Jesus before this earth life and that our Father in heaven loves us because He has sent us the Holy Ghost. May we all receive constant inspiration, direction and revelations from the Holy Ghost.

Chapter Sixteen

What Is Man?

The Parable of the Good Tree

A good tree bears good fruit and the fruit of that tree nourishes men as they grow in strength and health. And the master of the orchard comes and prunes the good trees that they might bear more good fruit.

But a bad tree does not bear good fruit and after many seasons of pruning the master of the orchard comes and cuts the tree down and casts it into the fire.

It is the same with man. A good man by his good works brings many souls to God. And the master of all men comes and quickens that man that he might do more good work and bring more souls unto God.

But an evil man after many seasons of bearing evil fruit and turning men away from God by his evil works is hewn down and cast into the fire.

The Psalmist has asked the question, "What is man, that thou art mindful of him? And the son of man, that thou visitest him? For thou hast made him a little lower than the angels, and hast crowned him with glory and honor" (Psalms 8:4-5).

Man is the supernal workmanship of the Almighty's hands. Man is God's greatest creation. So important is man to the Father's Plan of Salvation that without man, there would be no need for God. But man does exist and God does exist. All things were made by God-for the exaltation of man. The mission statement of God our beloved Father is, "This is my work and my glory, to bring to pass the immortality and eternal life of man" (Moses 1:39).

There is far more to man than man's natural eyes can see or the natural man's ears can hear or the mind of a natural man can understand. "But the natural man receiveth not the things of the Spirit of God: for they are foolishness unto him: neither can he know them, because they are spiritually discerned" (1 Corinthians 2:14). The things of God are spiritual and they must be spiritually discerned. "But there is a spirit in man and the inspiration of the Almighty giveth them understanding" (Job 32:8).

The question is, where did the spirit that is in man come from? The answer is, all things were made spiritually in heaven, before they were naturally upon the earth. "For I, the Lord God, created all things, of which I have spoken spiritually, before they were naturally upon the face of the earth" (Moses 3:5). "Nevertheless, all things were before created; but spiritually-were they created and made according to my word" (Moses 3:7). "And the Lord spake unto Enoch, and said unto him: Anoint thine eyes with clay and thou shalt see. And he did so. And he beheld the spirits that God had created; and he beheld also things which were not visible to the natural eye" (Moses 6:35-36).

What Is Man?

God has the blueprints to all things his hands have made. The Almighty has made millions of earths like the earth we live on. All of the creations of God are numbered unto him, "But only an account of this earth, and the inhabitants thereof, give I unto you. For behold, there are many worlds that have passed away by the word of my power. And there are many that now stand, and innumerable are they unto man; but all things are numbered unto me, for they are mine and I know them" (Moses 1:35).

"Behold, I am God; Man of Holiness is my name; Man of Council is my name; and endless and eternal is my name, also. Wherefore, I can stretch forth mine hands and hold all the creations which I have made; and mine eyes can pierce them also" (Moses 7:35-36).

"And Enoch said unto the Lord: How is it possible that thou canst weep, seeing thou art holy, and from all eternity to all eternity? And were it possible that man could number the particles of the earth, yea, millions of earths like this, it would not be a beginning to the number of thy creations, and thy curtains are stretched out still; and yet thou art there, and thy bosom is there; and also thou art just; thou art merciful and kind forever" (Moses 7:29-30).

A Part of Man Has Always Existed

Now let us go back farther, to the day God the Eternal Father stood in the midst of all unorganized matter. "Man was also in the beginning with God. Intelligence or the light of truth, was not created or made, neither indeed, can be" (D&C 93:29).

One day, God stood in the midst of all the intelligences, which have always existed and realized that the intelligence he possessed was greater than all the other intelligences combined. God thought it wise and prudent to clothe all of these intelligences in spirit matter.

The first of these to be born as a spirit child of the Father was Jesus Christ. On that day, God became a father. The spirit bodies of all those who would ever live on the earth followed. Therefore, all men and women are the literal spirit sons and daughters of our Heavenly Father.

Jesus Christ is literally our elder brother. We therefore, can all become heirs of God and joint heirs with Christ and inherit all the Father does possess. The apostle Paul spoke of this. Said he, "The Spirit itself beareth witness with our spirit, that we are the children of God: And if children, then heirs, heirs of God, and joint-heirs with Christ: If so be that we suffer with him, that we may be also glorified together" (Romans 8:16-17).

What Is Intelligence or the Light of Truth?

We cannot see intelligence with our natural eyes. Furthermore, God has not revealed to man what intelligence looks like. But when God the Eternal Father clothed man's intelligence; which has always existed, with spirit matter, which is also eternal, the spirit bodies and spirit identities of men were born.

"There is no such thing as immaterial matter. All spirit is matter, but it is more fine and pure and can only be discerned by purer eyes; We cannot see it; but when our bodies are purified we shall see that it is all matter" (D&C 131:7-8). That combination of intelligence and spirit matter which our beloved Heavenly Father first discovered and then organized, became the spirit bodies and spirit identities of man.

President Spencer W. Kimball wrote, "Our spirit matter was eternal and co-existent with

God, but it was organized into spirit bodies by our Heavenly Father" (Spencer W. Kimball, The Miracle of Forgiveness, p. 5, 1969, © Deseret Book Co, Used by Permission).

The Spirit Body of Man

The spirit body of man looks like the physical body of man. "The spirit of man is in the likeness of his person" (D&C 77:2).

"When the Savior shall appear we shall see him as he is. We shall see that he is a man like ourselves. And that same sociality which exists among us here shall exist among us there, only it will be coupled with eternal glory, which glory we do not now enjoy" (D&C 130: 1-2).

God the Eternal Father is the father of the spirit bodies of all men.

The Physical Body of Man

Adam was the first man to walk the earth, the first flesh (or man to posses a physical body) also. (See Moses 3:7)."And so it is written, the first man Adam was made a living soul; the last Adam was made a quickening spirit" (1 Cor. 15:45).

What Is Man?

I am aware of those who profess a belief in physical anthropology. I took a college course in that subject and read about those forms of man that many believe preceded Adam. They have the evidence they say, to make their case and they will show you the bones to prove it. But faith in Christ does not work that way. *The apostle Paul taught, "Now faith is the substance of things hoped for, the evidence of things that are not seen" (Hebrews 11:1).*

I wonder how many who believe other forms of man lived before Adam have prayed and asked God the Eternal Father to tell them who the first man on earth was? I hope you will ask God. If you do with faith, God will answer you. Remember, truth will hold up to any test. The truth stays the same yesterday, today and tomorrow. (See D&C 93:24).

I was not walking the earth when the first man Adam was. I did not have the privilege of being there and living with him. But Lucifer, or Satan who is the devil did visit Adam and Eve in the Garden of Eden. (See Genesis; Chapters, 2 and 3). Satan knows who the first man to walk this earth in a body of flesh and bones was.

Anyone witting about or teaching university classes professing that some other form of man preceded Adam has not the truth. This is a lie brought forth by the father of all lies even Satan, or the devil. (See, John 8:44).

Chapter Seventeen

Who Are You?

The Parable of the Three Trees

Three trees grew together in the same country. The fruit of the first tree was plentiful and it was pleasant to eat. People came from far away to eat the fruit: of that tree. And while the tree was yet alive the seeds of that tree were taken to many nations and planted. And many new trees grew to feed many people: of many nations. The second tree bore bitter fruit and the people who ate the fruit of that tree became sick and some died. In time, that tree was hewn down and cast into the fire. The third tree bore both sweet and bitter fruit. The people who ate the

Who Are You?

fruit of that tree were neither strengthened nor did they become sick. But they did become confused and they went off into forbidden paths and were lost.

Which tree represents your life?

What Are Your Talents?

Everyone, has been given at least one talent, by God, for the purpose of being successful in this life. I am not talking about what you may force yourself to do to earn a living. I'm talking about your talents. Are you serious about finding your talents? Answering these questions will help you find your talents: What do your friends say you do better than anyone else? What do you know you do better than anyone around you?

When you have those answers ask yourself two more questions: What do I love to do? What am I passionate about doing? When you answer all these questions you will have found your talents. What does the voice in your head keep whispering to you? What is it you may have kept a secret from everyone but have always wanted to do? Isn't it about time you made those old dreams of yours come true?

Man has got to learn to acquire a little courage and to conquer doubt and fear and do away with all those lame reasons folks will give you, for not getting anything done. All of those reasons and explanations and all of that rationalizing, is nothing more than excuses. But we must learn to say, "No excuse Sir!" and mean it. Then get out of that easy chair and get out there and just get it done!

Gifts of the Spirit

God has also given everyone a spiritual gift that all men and women might be reminded that the things of God are spiritual and that they must be spiritually discerned.

Some folks don't even know they have a spiritual gift but everyone has one. From the scripture we read, "But the manifestation of the Spirit is given to every man to profit withal. For to one is given by the Spirit the word of wisdom: to another the word of knowledge by the same Spirit: To another faith by the same Spirit: to another the gifts of healing by the same Spirit: To another the working of miracles: to another prophecy: to another discerning of spirits; to another divers kinds of tongues: to another the interpretation of tongues: But all these worketh that one and the selfsame Spirit, dividing to every man severally as he will" (1 Corinthians 12: 8-10).

Who Are You?

"For behold, to one is given by the Spirit of God, that he may teach the word of wisdom; And to another, that he may teach the word of knowledge by the same Spirit; And to another, exceeding great faith; and to another, the gifts of healing by the same Spirit; And again, to another, that he may work mighty miracles; And again to another, that he may prophesy concerning all things; And again, to another: the beholding of angels and ministering spirits; And again to another, all kinds of tongues; And again to another, the interpretation of languages and of divers kinds of tongues, And all these gifts come by the Spirit of Christ; and they come unto every man severally according as he will. And I would exhort you my beloved brethren, that you remember that every good gift cometh of Christ" (Moroni 10:8-18).

"To some it is given by the Holy Ghost to know that Jesus Christ is the Son of God, and that he was crucified for the sins of the world. To others it is given to believe on their words, that they also might have eternal life if they continue faithful. And again, to some it is give by the Holy Ghost to know the difference of administration, as it will be pleasing unto the same Lord, according as the Lord will, suiting his mercies according to the conditions of the children of men. And again it is given by the Holy Ghost to some to know the diversities of operations, whether they be of God, that the manifestations of the Spirit may be given to every man to profit withal. And again, verily I say unto you, to some is given, by the Spirit of God, the word of wisdom. To another is given the word of knowledge to be wise and to have knowledge. And again, to some it is given to have faith to be healed; And to others it is given to have faith to heal. And again to some is given the working of miracles; And to others it is given to prophesy; And to other the discerning of spirits.

And again, it is given to some to speak with tongues; And to another is given the interpretation of tongues. And all these gifts come from God, for the benefit of the children of God. And unto the bishop of the church, and unto such as God shall appoint and ordain to watch over the church and to be elders unto the church, are to have it given unto them to discern all those gifts lest there shall be any among you professing and yet be not of God. And it shall come to pass that he that asketh in Spirit shall receive in Spirit; That unto some it may be given to have all those gifts, that there may be a head, in order that ever member may be profited thereby" D&C 46:13-29).

Whatever your occupation may be, whatever country you may come from, whatever you hold in your heart as your core beliefs, there will always be one thing no man, neither the devil can ever take away from you: You are a

Who Are You?

child of God! God the Eternal Father is your father, Jesus Christ is your elder brother and all men and women who live on this earth are your brothers and sisters!

Chapter Eighteen

Who Is the Adversary?

The adversary is Lucifer. (Isaiah 14:12). Lucifer is yet another name title of the devil. The devil does exist. He is not the figment of anyone's imagination. The devil is also a spirit son of God the Eternal Father. "And Satan came among them, saying: I am also a son of God," (Moses 5:13). The devil is a spirit man made in the image and likeness of God the Eternal Father. Because of disobedience in the pre-existence neither the devil, nor his angels will ever take upon themselves physical bodies. They kept not their

Who Is the Adversary?

first estate. From the record of the prophet Abraham we have the following: "And we will prove them herewith, to see if they will do all things whatsoever the Lord their God shall command them; And they who keep their first estate shall be added upon; and they who keep not their first estate shall not have glory in the same kingdom with those who keep their first estate, and they who keep their second estate shall have glory added upon their heads for ever and ever. And the Lord said: Whom shall I send? And one answered like unto the Son of Man: Here am I, send me. And another answered and said: Here am I, send me. And the Lord said: I will send the first. And the second was angry and kept not his first estate, and, at that day, many followed after him" (Abraham 3:25-28).

The (second), spoken of by the prophet Abraham is Lucifer or the devil and (many who followed after him) are, one-third of the hosts of heaven.

The devil is our archenemy. The devil is committed with great intent, to drag all men quietly down to hell. From the Pearl of Great Price, we read: "And I, the Lord God, spake unto Moses, saying: That Satan, whom thou hast commanded in the name of mine Only Begotten, is the same which was from the beginning, and he came before me, saying-Behold, here am I, send me, I will be thy son, and I will redeem all mankind, that one soul shall not be lost, and surely I will do it; wherefore give me thine honor. But, behold, my Beloved Son, which was my Beloved and Chosen from the beginning said unto me-Father, thy will be done and the glory be thine forever. Wherefore, because that Satan rebelled against me, and sought to destroy the agency of man, which I, the Lord God had given him, and also, that I give unto him mine own power; by the power of min Only Begotten, I caused that the should be cast down. And he became Satan, yea, even the devil, *the father of* ALL LIES to deceive and to blind men, and to lead them captive at his will, even as many as would not hearken unto my voice" (Moses 4:1-4).

    You will notice that the scripture says, the devil is not the father of some lies but that the devil is the father of all lies. That means all lies were invented by the devil. No man ever told a lie that the devil did not first conceive. The devil is the great deceiver and liar. Satan appeared to Moses after he was visited by God and saw the glory of God. When visited by Satan, Moses quickly detected him. Moses asked, "Where is thy glory for it is darkness unto me? And I can judge between thee and God. Get thee hence Satan, deceive me not" (Moses 1:15). Moses is telling us something important here. Satan has no glory, no light, and no light of truth but only darkness about him. Satan told Moses, "I am the Only Begotten, worship me." (Moses 1:19). Thus, demonstrating once again that Satan is the great deceiver and the father of all lies.

The devil is the father of contention. "He that hath the spirit of contention is not of me, but is of the devil, who is the father of contention, and he stirreth up the hearts of men to contend with anger, one with another" (3 Nephi 11: 29). Man gets to choose to be angry or to be happy. Because Cain became angry with his brother Abel, the devil was given the opportunity to influence Cain further. Eventually, Cain chose to murder Abel. (Genesis 4: 1-16). The apostle Paul warned the Ephesians, "Be ye angry and sin not: let not the sun go down upon thy wrath: Neither give place to the devil" (Ephesians 4:26-27).

The devil is the great tempter. Satan was given leave by God to smite Job to see if Job would yield to temptation and curse God and die. (Job 1:6-21). "But in all this Job sinned not, nor charged God falsely" (Job 1:22). The devil even tempted Jesus Christ during his mortal ministry. (See Matthew 4:1-11). The third temptation of Satan was this: "Again the devil taketh him up into an exceeding high mountain, and sheweth him all the kingdoms of the world, and the glory of them; And saith unto him, All these things will I give thee, If thou wilt fall down and worship me. Then saith Jesus unto him, Get thee hence Satan, for it is written thou shalt worship the

Lord thy God, and him only shalt thou serve" (Matthew 4:8-10). Surely Satan will tempt all men. James has given us this instruction: "Resist the devil and he will flee from you" (James 4:7).

The devil can quote scripture (Matthew 4:1-11). The devil can appear as an angel of light. (D&C 129:8). The Lord has given us a test that we might know whether any administration is of God: "There are two kinds of beings in heaven, namely: Angels, who are resurrected personages, having bodies of flesh and bones-For instance, Jesus said: *Handle me and see, for a spirit hath not flesh and bones, as ye see me have.* Secondly: the spirits of just men made perfect, they who are not resurrected, but inherit the same glory. When a messenger comes saying he has a message from God, offer him your hand and request him to shake hands with you. If he be an angel he will do so, and you will feel his hand.

If he be the spirit of a just man made perfect he will come in his glory, for that is the only way he can appear-Ask him to shake hands with you, but he will not move, because it is contrary to the order of heaven for a just man to deceive; but he will still deliver his message. If it be the devil as an angel of light, when you ask him to shake hands he will offer you his hand, and you will not feel anything; you may therefore detect him. These are three grand keys whereby you may know if any administration is from God" (D&C 129: 1-9).

Who Is the Adversary?

The devil will do anything he can to keep men from coming unto Christ and doing good, for that is his mission: "But whatsoever thing persuadeth men to do evil and believe not in Christ, and deny him, and serve not God, then ye may know with a perfect knowledge it is of the devil; for after this manner doth the devil work, for he persuadeth no man to do good no, not one; neither do his angels, neither do they who subject themselves unto him" (Moroni 7:17).

Satan was not always, the devil. The devil began his life as a spirit son of God the Eternal Father. He obviously gained a position of authority in the pre-existence even enough to be called Lucifer; which means, "Light bearer" or the "Shining One." He was indeed, once "an angel in authority in the presence of God" (D&C 76:25-27). But because of disobedience, the devil and his angels were cast out of heaven and thrust down to the earth where they remain today. "And the great dragon was cast out, that old serpent, called the Devil and Satan, which deceiveth the whole world: he was cast out into the earth, and his angels were cast out with him" (Revelation 12:9).

The devil apparently, has great persuasive power because one third of the hosts of heaven elected to follow him. The devil is the god of this world, today. But his days of reining on the earth are limited. When the millennium begins, the devil and his angels will be cast into the bottomless pit for a thousand years, the length of the millennium. "And I saw an angel come down from heaven, having the key to the bottomless pit and a great chain in his hand. And he laid hold on the dragon, that old serpent, which is the Devil, and Satan, and bound him a thousand years, and cast him into the bottomless pit, and shut him up, and set a seal upon him that he should deceive the nations no more till the thousand years should be fulfilled: and after that he must be loosed a little season" (Revelation 20:1-3). When the millennial reign ends, the devil and his angles will be loosed for a season to tempt man. Jesus said of the devil, "he was a liar and a murderer from the beginning" (John 8:44)

Chapter Nineteen

I Don't Believe in God

"I don't believe in God," the man said. I answered, "isn't it about time you did?" "Not me, I don't believe in anything I cannot see!" That is a most interesting statement for me to hear. Do you not know that God is all around you everyday of your life? I saw God just the other day in a grocery store. I had just driven there following a visit to the Provo, temple. I had met a young married couple there and now they were in the grocery store with their newborn babe in a bassinet. I said hello to the parents and then walked up to the newborn babe. Before I could get there, the little guy was almost sitting up to greet me. I leaned down and looked deeply into the little fella's eyes. The spirit within the little boy almost leaped out of his body with excitement. This precious little child recognized me and I recognized him. He was just in the presence of God and angels a few weeks earlier and his little spirit still remembered his Heavenly Father.

I saw God just a few summer's ago on a business trip while driving across New Mexico on my way to Santa Fe. I pulled off the Interstate at about 3 AM and found a safe place to rest for awhile and when I got out of the car, I looked up into the night sky and I saw God moving about the Milky Way Galaxy in his majesty and glory.

The stars were so clear on that night and they seemed to be so close; I felt I could reach out my hands and touch them. NASA tells us in the year (2016) that there are from 100 to 400 billion stars in the Milky Way Galaxy and it seemed to me that I was seeing most all of them on that night! (From Wikipedia, NASA Blueshift, Archived from the original on January 25, 2016).

I saw and heard God on one autumn day in the parking lot of another place I shop. On that afternoon, I sat in my car for more than 20 minutes and watched and listened to a thunder and lightning storm that no one could easily forget.

The thunder filled my ears and lightning flashed across the entire eastern sky in a brilliant display of awesome power and energy and I soon realized I was watching God move about in his majesty and glory. We read from the revelations God has given modern man: "The earth rolls upon her wings, and the sun giveth his light by day, and the moon giveth her light by night, and the stars also give their light, as they roll upon their wings in their glory, in the midst of the power of God. Unto what shall I liken these kingdoms, that ye may understand?

"Behold, all these are kingdoms, and any man who hath seen any or the least of these hath seen God moving in his majesty and power" (D&C 88: 45-47).

God lives! There is no escaping that reality. But how can I find this out for myself, you may ask? There is a way and it has stayed the same since our first parents, Adam and Eve were on the earth. When Adam and Eve were cast out of the Garden of Eden, Adam built an altar to pray, to commune with God. That is what we all must do. We simply need to pray. We need to speak with God. We need only to ask God if he lives and God will not fail to answer us.

Jesus said, "Ask, and it shall be given you; seek, and ye shall find; knock, and it shall be opened unto you:

For every one that asketh receiveth: and he that seeketh findeth: and to him that knocketh it shall be opened" (Matthew 7:7-8). "And all things whatsoever ye ask in prayer, believing, ye shall receive" (Matthew 21:22).

This promise is unto all, "Be thou humble: and the Lord thy God shall lead thee by the hand, and give thee answer to thy prayers" (D&C 112:10).

Chapter Twenty

I Am Not Religious

Going to church every Sunday and sitting on one of the prominent and visible pews does not make you religious. Some of the most religious people I know do not belong to any church. Some of the good people of the world seldom go to church. But these are the people who are constantly helping their neighbors and family and friends, often without being asked. But when they are asked to help, they are always the first to show up.

Jesus wants all of us to remember the Sabbath day to keep it holy and a big part of the way we do that is by attending church. But if we only go to church to be seen of others our church going isn't doing us much good.

I was talking to two middle aged gentlemen a while back and they immediately said, "I am not religious." The first man said, "I do not go to church every Sunday and I do not belong to any church so I am not religious."

So I asked him, "do you help your family and friends when they ask for help and do you stop to help someone on the highway who may have car or truck trouble and needs help? "I do that all the time," he said. "I believe if you help people, expecting nothing in return, then you are religious! " I read what James has told us pure religion is to them: *"Pure religion and undefiled before God and the Father is this, to visit the fatherless and widows in their affliction and to keep himself unspotted from the world" (James 1:27).*

"Now I've got you," one of them said. "I don't visit the fatherless and widows in their affliction." The first man said. I said, "Perhaps the only reason you do not is because you did not know that would be a good thing to do." Then I explained, the fatherless are not just orphans; they include young and old men and women who now live alone without a living father and mother. We already know who widows are but why has the Lord brought the plight of such to our attention?

Christ is teaching us that the fatherless and widows need more attention in this life than others because they are among the most neglected and forgotten people in the world. Now that you know the importance of helping the fatherless and the widows in their affliction and who they are; I am certain that any man who would help a family member, a neighbor or a friend when he calls would also help the fatherless and widows of the world.

Then I asked them, "Do you keep yourself unspotted from the world?"

"Now that's where I've got you for sure, the first man answered. "When I was a young man I did some powerful bad things and there's no getting around that."

"Do you still do those powerful bad things?" "No sir, those days are long gone." "Everybody makes mistakes," said the man standing by him. "Amen to that brother," said the first man.

"Let me show you what the Savior of the world had to say about a man who admits he has made mistakes and then stops doing what he knows is wrong. Jesus said: "By this ye may know if a man repenteth of his sins-behold, he will confess them and forsake them" (D&C 58:43).

That is what you just did. You talked about your mistakes and you put your mistakes behind you. The Bible has something to say about this very thing: "He that covereth his sins shall not prosper: but whoso confesseth and forsaketh them shall have mercy" (Proverbs 28:13).

Then I said, it seems to me that you may be a little more religious than the fella who goes to church and says one thing about what he believes but may be secretly doing some powerful bad things.

"Well how about that!" The man said.

If you would like to read about what Jesus had to say about hypocrites, take a look at *Chapter 31: What Do I Have To Do To Get To Heaven?* There is another requirement for being religious but most folks are not aware of this: "If any among you seem to be religious, and bridleth not his tongue, but deceiveth his own heart, that man's religion is vain" (James 1:26). It is a wise man, who considers the words that begin to form in his mind before they reach the tip of his tongue and leave his mouth. Once those words are spoken, you can never call them back.

Be still and ask this question, "Will my words hurt or injure anyone? Ask yourself, will my words demean another or will my words lift the other person up?"

I Am Not Religious

If you don't have anything good to say about someone do not say anything. Speaking evil of another can lead to gossip. Gossip will inevitably lead to slander and slander can lead to bearing false witness of thy neighbor. When you have done that, you have broken one of God's Ten Commandments. The commandment is, "Thou shalt not bear false witness against thy neighbor" (Exodus 20:16).

"Speak not evil one of another, brethren. He that speaketh evil of his brother, speaketh evil of the law; but if thou judge the law thou art not a doer of the law, but a judge. There is one lawgiver who is able to save and destroy: who art thou that judgest another" (James 4:11-12)?

There is an old playground saying that children learn: "Sticks and stones can break my bones but words will never hurt me." Sounds good, but words can hurt people. Words can devastate another person. Man has laws in place to punish those who use words to demean or drag others down and to manipulate the self worth of others. "Mental Cruelty" is in place.

For some young men and women who find themselves in grade school, the school bully is an ongoing nuisance. But the school bully is usually guilty of physical abuse. Little is said of the school bully who hurts others with his words.

The gospel of Jesus Christ teaches us to build people up and not to knock them down. People who say things to intentionally hurt other people's feelings such as, "you're no good. You're worthless." I'm better than you," are people who usually have low self-esteem and rely on such behavior to build themselves up, by knocking another person down.

Jesus had something to say on this subject, Said he, "But I say unto you, that whosoever is angry with his brother without a cause shall be in danger of the judgment: and whosoever shall say unto his brother Raca, (worthless) shall be in danger of the council: but whosoever shall say thou fool, shall be in danger of hell fire" (Matthew 5:22; emphasis added).

The word, raca (Smith) is a term of reproach derived from the Chaldee language (reka) which means, worthless. "Raca denotes a certain looseness of life and manner, while fool, in the same passage, means a downright wicked and reproachable person."

The word, Raca (EBD) means: Vain, empty, worthless, and is only found in (Matthew 5:22). The Jews used it as a word of contempt. It is derived from a root meaning "to spit." An Aramaic term of contempt and abuse, which means, 'empty one'. Jesus taught: But let your communication be, Yea, yea; Nay, nay: for whatsoever is more than these cometh of evil" (Matthew 5:37).

Chapter Twenty-One

I Am Not Worthy

The Parable of the Complaining and Impatient Man

There was a certain man who got down on his knees and prayed with his lips and in his heart every day: O God the Eternal Father, I thank thee for the air I breathe. Thank you for the talents you have given me and for the gifts of the Spirit you have given me. I ask that thou wilt extend my days that I might be able to finish all thou has sent me here on earth to do that I might bring more souls unto thee, on earth and in heaven and that I might continue to give all the honor and glory to thee. And the God of heaven quickened that man by the power of the Spirit and gave that man more talents and more gifts of the Spirit.

Another man complained in his prayers and troubled God constantly with the same prayers. God, I ask thee to bless me with more talents and gifts of the Spirit that I might some day bring souls unto thee like this man who brings souls to thee. Why do I not have his talents and gifts of the Spirit? And after a long period of time the Lord answered that man.

And the voice of the Spirit of God came into the man's mind and said: "Son you have not understood. You have supposed that your Father gives talents and gifts of the Spirit to men just for the asking. You must search out and find the talents and gifts of the Spirit you already have: for all men have been given some. Then you must come before thy maker and admit your weaknesses and ask God to humble you that you might understand the things of God.

Then you must magnify the talents and gifts of the Spirit you already have. Then if God finds you worthy you will be blessed in God's time with more. But blessings will come in the wisdom of God's time and timing, and not your own timing and only if you are found worthy.

It has been a rare occasion indeed, when I have heard the words: "I am not worthy" spoken to me in the context of drawing near to Almighty God or entering the kingdom of heaven.

I Am Not Worthy

It has been my great privilege to teach the gospel of Jesus Christ to hundreds of people in my lifetime and yet I have no memory of anyone ever saying to me, "I am not worthy" pertaining to receiving the blessings of God, with the exception of my own brother.

Men are not in the habit of saying, "I am not worthy" to build themselves up or to make another think better of them. On the contrary, when a man says he is not worthy in the context of heavenly things, he is acknowledging that he has faults. He is suggesting that he needs to improve himself and to repent. But we all have faults, we all have weaknesses and we all need to improve ourselves and to repent.

Jesus Christ is the only perfect man to ever walk this earth. "For all have sinned, and come short of the glory of God" (Romans 3:23).

But the Lord has said: "If men come unto me I will show unto them their weakness. I give unto men weakness that they may be humble; and my grace is sufficient for all men that humble themselves before me; for if they humble themselves before me, and have faith in me, then will I made weak things become strong unto them" (Ether 12: 27).

In addition to this, all men can become worthy to enter into the kingdom of heaven because of the perfect and infinite atonement of Jesus Christ. What a wonderful thing it is to know that the debt has been paid for our sins!

The price has been paid for the sins of all mankind. During the Savior's mortal ministry there were two instances recorded in scripture (pertaining to men becoming worthy to enter the kingdom of God) when men said or implied and demonstrated: *I am not worthy:* The publican who smote upon his breast while he stood and prayed: "And the publican, standing afar off, would not lift up so much as his eyes unto heaven, but smote upon his breast, saying, God be merciful to me a sinner" (Luke 18 13). When a man says, "I am not worthy," whether he realizes it or not he is also saying there is something greater than I am out there. The publican said, "God have mercy upon me, a sinner" (Luke 18:13).

The centurion sent his friends to Jesus before Jesus could reach his house and instructed them to say: "Lord trouble not thyself: for I am not worthy that thou shouldest enter under my roof: Wherefore neither thought myself worthy to come unto thee: but say in a word, and my servant shall be healed. For I am also a man set under authority, having under me soldiers, and I say unto one, Go, and he goeth; and to another, Come, and he cometh: and to my servant, Do this and he doeth it" (Luke 7:8).

Clearly the centurion was a good man. He was concerned enough for the welfare of even the servant he loved, that he sought Jesus out. He had no doubt, heard of Jesus healing others and

I Am Not Worthy

he had faith that Jesus could heal his servant by only speaking the word," be thou healed" from afar off. He would not risk offending Jesus by having him enter his home because in saying, he was not worthy, he also implied and perhaps knew very well, that he was a sinner.

The record continues: "When Jesus heard these things, he marveled at him, and turned him about, and said unto the people that followed him, I say unto you, I have not found so great faith, no, not in Israel" (Luke 7:9).

To all those who say, "I am not worthy" whether you realize it or not, you have already taken the first step to becoming, worthy.

In times of old it was the firstling of a flock of sheep that was required as a sacrifice, symbolizing the sacrifice of Jesus Christ as a lamb without spot and without blemish to be offered as a sacrifice to atone for the sins of the world. A broken heart and a contrite spirit is now required as man's sacrifice.

The natural man will always be an enemy to God. (See Mosiah 3:19). But when man realizes he is not worthy and is willing to submit himself to the will of God and not his own will, that man can certainly become worthy to return to live with God in heaven again forever.

Chapter Twenty-Two

There Are Too Many Translations of the Bible

One of my customers whom I have yet to meet in person but have taken his orders over the phone for more than twenty years taught me something I did not know about the Bible. We were recently having a pleasant conversation and I mentioned some reference to the Bible. He asked me, "what translation of the Bible are you talking about, there are many translations of the Bible." His words caused me to do a little research. According to Wikipedia, the free encyclopedia, there are 104 versions or translations of the complete Bible in English.

There Are Too Many Translations of the Bible

There are 18 incomplete Bible translations in English and 33 Partial Bible translations in English. "As of November 2014 the full Bible has been translated into 531 languages, and 2,883 languages have at least some portion of the Bible."

How many languages are spoken in the world today? The 2005 edition of Ethnologue lists 6,912 living languages from 885 million native speakers of Mandarin in 12 countries to the Coos language spoken by one or two people in Southern Oregon.

From the first Gutenberg Bible printed in November of 1444 until 2014 there have been more than 6 billion Bibles sold, making the Bible the best selling book of all time! If you were able to read the 104 translations of the complete Bible that have been translated into English at the rate of one each month it would take you 8.66667 years to read all 104 translations. There is an easier way. How can anyone know which translation of the Bible is the one containing what God intended it to contain? If you will pray and ask God, you can know the truth of all things by the power of the Holy Ghost. (See Moroni 10:5). A child will understand this but not an intellectual. The intellectual will be, "ever learning and never able to come to a knowledge of the truth" (II Timothy 3:7).

"We believe the Bible to be the word of God as far as it is translated correctly. We also believe the Book of Mormon to be the word of God" (Eighth Article of Faith) of the Church of Jesus Christ of Latter-day Saints. I have always used this scripture as my guide: "Everything which inviteth to do good, and to persuade to believe in Christ is sent forth by the power and gift of Christ; wherefore ye may know with a perfect knowledge it is from God" (Moroni 7:16). The Savior told us: "All things are written by the Father" (3 Nephi 27:26). If we change or alter or leave out too many of the Father's words, we could change the meaning of the Father's words.

I do not know what version or translation of the Bible young Joseph Smith was reading when he found the verse in the book of James that motivated him to pray to God. I do know that the same verse he quotes in his testimony from the book of James is in my King James translation of the Bible and they match the words Joseph uses in his testimony, word for word flawlessly. Young Joseph read: "If any of you lack wisdom, let him ask of God, that giveth to all men liberally, and upraideth not; and it shall be given him" (James 1:5).

I am more interested in the effect of young Joseph reading those words in his Bible. Had he not read the words of James in his Bible, young Joseph Smith may have never gone into the woods to find a quiet place to kneel down

There Are Too Many Translations of the Bible

and pray and ask God which of all the churches he should join: *"My object in going to inquire of the Lord was to know which of all the sects was right, that I might know which to join. No sooner, therefore, did I get possession of myself, so as to be able to speak, than I asked the Personages who stood above me in the light, which of all the sects was right-and which I should join. I was answered that I must join none of them, for they were all wrong: and the Personage who addressed me said that all their creeds were an abomination in his sight; that those professors were all corrupt; that: "they draw near to me with their lips, but their hearts are far from me, that they teach for doctrine the commandments of men, having a form of godliness but denying the power thereof."* (Joseph Smith 2:18-19).

Chapter Twenty-Three

There Are Too Many Churches from Which to Choose

His Religion Is Not My Religion

Copyright © 2017 by Ron Bartalini
From the album Supernova/Ron Bartalini

But his religion is not my religion.

There Are Too Many Churches from Which to Choose

What he believes is not what I believe at all.
But his religion is not my religion.
What he believes is not what I believe at all.
Now I know I am supposed to love him.
And when I love him, I understand him after all.
But his religion is not my religion.
What he believes is not what I believe at all.
But his religion is not my religion.
What he believes is not what I believe at all.
Don't be dismayed. Many men will be different than you.
No matter what color his skin is: All men are brothers after all.
But his religion is not my religion.
What he believes is not what I believe at all.
But his religion is not my religion.
What he believes is not what I believe at all.
Now I know I am supposed to love him.
And when I love him, I understand him after all.

    How many Christian churches are there out there? According to the Center for the Study of Global Christianity (CSGC) at Gordon-Conwell Theological Seminary, there are approximately 41,000 Christian denominations and organizations in the world.
    This statistic takes into consideration cultural distinctions of denominations in different countries, so there is overlapping of

many denominations. (Center For The Study of: Global Christianity 2011).

Perhaps one should ask, how many versions, adaptations, alterations and re-inventions are there, of the only true and living Church of Jesus Christ, which is the church Christ founded during his mortal ministry? The question would also arise quite quickly: How can all these churches possibly be the one and only true Church of Jesus Christ? The answer is clear. They cannot.

When Joseph Smith was fourteen years old, he prayed and asked God which of all the churches he should join. He was told he should join none on them: *"My object in going to inquire of the Lord was to know which of all the sects was right, that I might know which to join. No sooner, therefore, did I get possession of myself, so as to be able to speak, than I asked the Personages who stood above me in the light, which of all the sects was right—and which I should join. I was answered that I must join none of them, for they were all wrong: and the Personage who addressed me said that all their creeds were an abomination in his sight; that those professors were all corrupt; that: "they draw near to me with their lips, but their hearts are far from me, that they teach for doctrine the commandments of men, having a form of godliness but denying the power thereof."* "He again forbad me to join with any of them; and *many other things did he say unto me which I cannot write at this time" (Joseph Smith 2: 18-20).*

My Conversion to The Church of Jesus Christ of Latter-day Saints

The following story was given to me by one of my neighbors. I have asked his permission to include it within this book.

"I only recall going one time to a Methodist Church when I was growing up in Long Beach, California. My father was not a religious person but my mother on the other hand was very interested in religion having attended several different churches in her youth.

For some reason though, in her early adult years she had lost faith in organized religion and so by the time I came around attending church services was not something we did as a family. However, we did spend time together on Sundays at the golf course! At some point, I think I was maybe 12, I decided to stay home on Sundays when my parents left to golf. By this time, both of my sisters had moved out of our home, thus leaving me alone when my parents were gone.

Both of my parents drank heavily in my growing up years. My mother later would admit to being an alcoholic (my father never would). Because of their drinking, the liquor cupboard in our home was always well stocked. I remember that at age 12, on Sundays while my parents were golfing (which was a five to six hour event), I got into the liquor cupboard and began drinking myself.

As part of my dad's work my parents often had to go to social functions in the evenings where drinking was the norm, and more often than not they would come home late and drunk. To add to this sad situation, they were not getting along in my early teenage years and thus the drinking got heavier and the fighting was horrible! In looking back, I have wondered why I began to drink at such an early age and why it escalated to three to four times a week (and to get drunk also). I'm sure I was escaping the constant drama and sadness so prevalent in my home at that time. However, I do not want to paint my parents as awful drunks and lousy parents...I really didn't know any different and I always felt loved-they just had drinking problems, no religion, and a strained relationship. My drinking got worse and by the 9th grade I fear I was on my own path to addiction!

There Are Too Many Churches from Which to Choose

On one summer evening, I drank so much that I was taken to my friend's home and his mother (a nurse) cared for me all night. I remember the next morning they told me I needed to go home…that my dad wanted to take me on a trip to Clovis, California (near Fresno). I also remember being so sick on that flight! My dad really wasn't taking me on a flight, he was teaching me a lesson (he knew about my drinking) and he was going to have me work on some acreage he owned where he was planting pistachios. It was a miserable week with temperatures above 100 degrees every day, all the while I strung barbed-wire fencing! However, something happened to me while I had all of that alone time in the "fields."

Shortly after returning from Clovis I started having some very interesting yearnings! For some reason, I decided I needed religion (which I'm sure had something to do with my drinking and my parents' drinking and fighting). Sometime in the fall of 1970, when I was 14 years old, a friend and I decided to put on our ties, get on our bicycles and try out different churches.

I remember the first Sunday arriving at a certain church very early in the morning before their meeting started. We waited on the steps of the church until the people arrived. That day I know we attended the services of a couple of churches.

I continued this effort for weeks, attending numerous different churches (including their weeknight youth meetings). I remember that my friend dropped his quest for religion after a week or two. I think back on this and realize how amazing it was for a young 14 year old to be riding around Long Beach on his bicycle checking out different religions!

Well, after a month or two of searching and never finding anything that appealed to me (some scared me, some seemed disorganized and others confused me), I was standing on my front lawn when a junior high school friend came riding by on his bicycle. I asked him where he was going, to which he replied, "church." I asked if I could join him and of course he was excited! The meetinghouse for The Church of Jesus Christ of Latter-day Saints was actually the closest church building to my home but I never did think of attending one of their meetings because when I was younger, we always walked to our elementary school through the parking lot of the LDS Church until one day a young friend said that her mom no longer wanted her to walk through the church parking lot because those people were "weird."

My friend, Kevin, and I attended a weeknight youth gathering called "Mutual." I cannot remember anything remarkable about that evening (as I recall we played volleyball), but

There Are Too Many Churches from Which to Choose

I felt something that I didn't feel in any of the other churches. I immediately wanted to be a part of what I was experiencing and I asked Kevin how someone could become a "Mormon?" He said, "he'd have the missionaries come see me!"

The interesting thing that occurred once I told my parents about what I had been doing, (my experience at the Mormon Church and how I wanted to join the Church), was how indifferent they were at the time to me doing so. Possibly because of all that was going on in their lives at the time or for whatever reason, their hearts were softened and they allowed me to listen to the missionaries in our home.

I look back on this as a miracle because my mom, who years later decided to join the Catholic Church, said that if she had known what a life-long commitment my religion would become she probably wouldn't have consented to my baptism (even though she acknowledges how great the Church has been for me and my family). I was baptized a member of The Church of Jesus Christ of Latter-day Saints on February 11, 1971.

I have often wondered why a young man, like myself, would be so interested in joining a church. I know that countless thousands have searched for religion in their youth, but nevertheless I look back upon it as one of the greatest blessings of my life. Why did I feel the need (except for the obvious desire to change some of the circumstances of my life)? Was I prompted or prodded by others from the other side of the veil? A few years after my baptism I received a patriarchal blessing wherein the Patriarch said in the blessing that when I joined the Church there were many of my ancestors in the spirit world rejoicing. Might they have prompted and prodded me along? I discovered later that one of my ancestors, a Reverend John Lathrop, was also a forefather of Joseph Smith, Jr., Wilford Woodruff, Lorenzo Snow, George Albert Smith, Harold B. Lee and others. Might the Reverend Lathrop have been one prompting and prodding one of his descendants to discover the true gospel of Jesus Christ? I do not know. I do know that being a member of The Church of Jesus Christ of Latter-day Saints is the greatest blessing of my life! The gospel of Jesus Christ has blessed both me and my family and hopefully thousands of others with whom I have associated throughout my life."

Chapter Twenty-Four

I Will Continue to Follow the Traditions of the Fathers

It is the unwritten duty of man to question everything. If a thing is true it will pass the test of cross-examination. If a thing is true it will stay true forever. "For truth is knowledge of things as they are, and as they were, and as they are to come" (D&C 93:24).

But to find the truth, one must go back further than the tradition of the fathers. One must go back further than one or two or even four thousand years. One must go way back before our earthly fathers, even father Adam began.

To find pure and unadulterated truth one must go back to the beginning. To find pure truth, one must go back to before Lucifer became the devil and had time and opportunity to pollute, the pure and unadulterated truth. To find the pure truth, one must go back to when we lived with God in heaven.

When mankind began as spirit sons and daughters of God, all were innocent. We read: "Every spirit of man was innocent in the beginning; and God having redeemed men from the fall, men became again, in their infant state, innocent before God. And that wicked one cometh and taketh away light and truth through disobedience, from the children of men, *and because of the tradition of their fathers.* But I have commanded you to bring up your children in light and truth" (D&C 93:37-39).

Our father Adam taught his children light and truth and he taught them of the ways of God. But the devil came tempting and said unto Adam's children, "believe it not, and they believed it not" (Moses 5:13).

We read from the account of Moses found

in the Pearl of Great Price: "And Adam blessed the name of God, and they made all things known unto their sons and their daughters. And Satan came among them, saying: I am also a son of God, and he commanded them saying:
Believe it not; and they believed it not, and they loved Satan more than God. And men began from that time forth to be carnal, sensual, and devilish" (Moses 5:12-13).

Abraham's father was an idolater. One of the priests from that religion was about to sacrifice Abraham to idol gods but an angel of the true and living God came to save Abraham's life. If Abraham followed, the tradition of his father, he would not have become a great prophet of Almighty God. There would have been no Abraham, Isaac and Jacob. Neither would there have been Joseph: the son of Jacob, who was sold into Egypt from which Ephraim and Manasseh sprang.

The Lord has given us a spiritual definition of truth: "And truth is a knowledge of things as they are, and as they were and as they are to come" (D&C 93:24).

You will notice that truth stays the same throughout time. Before you blindly follow the tradition of your fathers, ask Almighty God if those traditions are true. If they are true, they will stand the test of an honest cross-examination. The truth will continue to be the truth but one must go back to the beginning to find it.

On the other hand, if you follow the tradition of your fathers, which may turn out to be false, you could spend your life moving farther and farther away from God until you no longer believe in God at all. Put all tradition to the test. Ask God and God will answer you by the power of the Holy Ghost. The Holy Ghost will reveal the truth of all things to you.

Please remember how father Adam's children lost light and truth: *"And that wicked one cometh and taketh away light and truth through disobedience, from the children of men and by the tradition of their fathers"* (D&C 93:37-38).

"For behold, again I say unto you, that if ye will enter in by the way, and receive the Holy Ghost, it will show unto you all things what ye should do" (2 Nephi 32:5).

"And by the power of the Holy Ghost, ye may know the truth of all things" (Moroni 10:5).

Chapter Twenty-Five

I Am Too Old to Change

As long as you are alive and breathing, you are not too old to change for the better forever!

Sister Amanda Clearwater who served her mission in Chile just returned home a short time ago. She has given me this story to share:

"One of the most incredible people I met while serving my mission in Chile was a 90 year-old man. He had been stubbornly avoiding baptism all his life. His name is Hugo Gonzales and his wife and son were baptized more than 40 years ago. They were among the pioneers of the members of the Church of Jesus Christ of Latter-day Saints in Chile. Hugo basically lived the gospel. He did not attend church but other than that, he knew a lot of the doctrines. One of his favorite doctrines was baptism for the dead. He actually had this idea engraved in his mind, that when he died, his son was going to do his baptism for him in the temple. That is how he was going to find his salvation. He was going to get baptized after he was dead. For forty years this is what he believed!

The week before I showed up in his ward, the sister missionaries, were visiting the Gonzales family. The subject of Hugo being baptized vicariously by his son Rene came up in the conversation. Hugo's son asked his father then, "wouldn't it be more special if you were to be baptized in life, what are we waiting for? He also mentioned, that his daughter was turning eight years old in two weeks and she will need to be baptized. Eight years old is the age children can be baptized. Hugo's son Rene asked, "What if we made this a very special occasion for you and for her?"

He didn't respond at that time but he was left pondering the question. The next week I showed up at his house and he left us with this statement: "O.K., I'm going to get baptized." So we started teaching him the gospel of Jesus Christ. It was kind of hard for him. He was very faithful and very believing but there were a few things that he said, "I don't know about this." But then he would stop and say, "I'm an old man, I've been stubborn for this long, I really feel like this is what I should do, so I'm going to let this go." He was learning so fast. I was shocked at how fast he was learning for a 90 year old man. Generally, our ability to remember things and grow kind of stops after a certain time. But he was learning and growing as he learned different doctrines. He stopped drinking tea after 90 years of drinking tea. His prayers were the sweetest things I have ever heard in my entire life. Every time he prayed, he was asking questions. He was just kind of conversing with his Father. He asked to understand things better and he was declaring, this is what he was going to do. He prayed, "this is what I believe you want me to do and I will do whatever you ask." I think of that kind of faith, I haven't seen a better example of faith in my entire life. Here is a man who had the gospel in front of him all of his life, but when he finally decided to take this step, there is nothing that could have changed him. Soon after this, this 90 year-old man entered into the waters of baptism letting his youngest son baptize him.

    There was such a sweet spirit that day. His wife who has Alzheimer's was there at his baptism as well. There were so many times that he wanted her to understand that he was getting baptized. She kind of didn't understand it at first. But the week before his baptism she said to us, "guess what, he's getting baptized!" And she remembered. He said the closing prayer at his baptism and he thanked the Lord for that. And I think, those small things are the most important."

Another neighbor of mine just told me about a 92 old woman he baptized while serving his mission. While in the Provo temple last year I sat next to a man who told me that day was his 100th birthday!

The oldest verified person ever was French woman Jeanne Calment, who died at the age of 122 years, 164 days. The oldest living person as of May 23, 2015 is Jeralean Talley born 23 May 1899 who is 116 years and 17 days old and living in the United States. (From Wikipedia: the free encyclopedia).

You can never be too old to change your life for the better forever.

Chapter Twenty-Six

What Do I Have to Do to Get to Heaven?

The smallest act of kindness will do more to get you to heaven than you may ever understand in this life. But many acts of kindness will infuse your soul with the light of Christ and you will then be able to see clearly to make your way back to heaven. Jesus Christ was the only perfect man to walk this earth but if we can learn to love even little worms, then it will be a lot easier to love our neighbors. The following song was written for children but there is something there for all:

Don't Hurt Worms

Copyright © 2017 by Ron Bartalini
From Lollipop Molly Songs/Ron Bartalini

Don't hurt worms. Worms are our friends.
Even little worms need some love now and then.
They have troubles enough with the birds eating them. So please—Don't hurt worms.
And when you see them on the sidewalk
after a long hard rain—
Just give them a little nudge
back on the grass again.
Don' hurt worms. Worms are our friends.
Even little worms need some love now and then.
They have troubles enough
with the birds eating them.
so please—Don't hurt worms.
Are you only human or are you also humane?
So please---Don't hurt worms. You know you love them.
Don't hurt—little wormy wormers.

Family Is the Key to Eternal Life

    The family is the key to eternal happiness and eternal life. The first commandment God gave to Adam and Eve was to "multiply and replenish the earth" (Genesis 1:28).

What Do I Have to Do to Get to Heaven?

A family that lives the gospel of Jesus Christ will have love in their family and they will have love for their neighbors and since love is the heart of the gospel of Jesus Christ the family that loves all God's hands have made will find their way back to God to live with God in heaven forever!

Making a list of what you should do and not do, to get to heaven is not going to get you to heaven. What if the person making the list leaves out something important? What if you fail to do or not do, everything on the list?

What you will need is one thing that will cover everything you have to do, if you do that one thing. And here it is: Love is the answer to everything. Not just love alone but loving God and all that God's hands have made, is the answer to everything.

The first great commandment is this: "Thou shalt love the Lord thy God with all thy heart and with all thy soul and with all thy mind" (Matthew 22:37).

But how do we love God in this way?

God does not want just part of your heart and part of your soul and part of your mind. The Lord God made all of your heart and all of your soul and all, of your mind and He wants it all back. If you give God just a part of your heart, soul and mind you will be cheating God and cheating yourself, out of blessings that could be yours.

The scripture says: "I know thy works, that thou art neither cold nor hot: I would that thou wert cold or hot. So because thou art lukewarm, and neither cold nor hot, I will spue thee out of my mouth" (Revelation 3: 15-16).

There is only one way to love God and that is to understand that in order to love God we must first love our neighbor.

"And the second (great commandment) is this: "Thou shalt love thy neighbor as thyself" (Matthew 22:39).

Who is our neighbor? Everyone on earth: besides-yourself. John the Beloved has given us the grand key to knowing how to love God.

Here it is: "If a man say, I love God, and hateth his brother, he is a liar; for he that loveth not his brother whom he hath seen, how can he love God who he hath not seen? And this commandment we have from him. That he who loveth God love his brother also" (1 John 4:20-21).

How Do I Get to Heaven?

I will only give you the answers Jesus gave in the Holy Scriptures: "Blessed are the poor in spirit, for theirs is the kingdom of heaven" (Matthew 5:3).

What does the phrase, "poor in spirit," mean? In our day, this means: to have a broken heart and a contrite spirit, to be aware of one's weaknesses, to be teachable, to be humble.

Wo unto you poor men, whose hearts are not broken, whose spirits are not contrite: (D&C 56:17).

Therefore, we see that to just be poor or without worldly riches is not enough to get us into heaven.

"Blessed are they which are persecuted for righteousness' sake for theirs is the kingdom of heaven" (Matthew 5:10). "Blessed are ye, when men shall revile you and persecute you, and shall say all manner of evil against you falsely, for my sake. Rejoice, and be exceeding glad: for great is your reward in heaven" (Matthew 5:11-12).

"For God so loved the world that he gave His only begotten Son that whosoever believeth on him should not perish but have everlasting life" (John 3:16).

One Must Believe in Christ

"He that believeth on the Son hath everlasting life and he that believeth not on the Son shall not see life but the wrath of God abideth on him" (John 3:35-36).

Faith in Jesus Christ is the first principle of the gospel of Jesus Christ. To have faith in money and riches or to have faith in your favorite sports team or movie star or rock star or Olympic athlete or even to have faith in your retirement portfolio or your own company or the five star company you have always invested in will not get you to heaven. To have faith in Jesus Christ will get you to heaven and an abiding faith in Jesus Christ will help you to endure until the end.

"And this is life eternal, that they might know thee, the only true God and Jesus Christ whom thou hast sent" (John 17:3).

One Must Know and Love God

If a man truly knows God, he will love God. Why? Because God's commandments are designed to uplift man and take man back to heaven to live with the Father and the Son forever. If a man loves God, that man will keep God's commandments and endure until the end. Loving God allows a man to know God and knowing God allows a man to love God. That is the way it works.

"Not everyone that saith unto me, Lord, Lord shall enter into the kingdom of heaven but he that doeth the will of my Father which is in heaven" (Matthew 7:21).

What Do I Have to Do to Get to Heaven?

What is the will of the Father for all mankind? Answer: That we offer God a broken heart and a contrite spirit, that we admit our weaknesses to God. That we become teachable and humble, willing to submit to all things the Father may inflict upon us. But mainly, that we allow God to change our hearts, to soften our hearts that we might choose to make the will of God our own will.

Repentance Is Required

Repentance is required to enter the kingdom of heaven. To the Saints, on the American continent following his resurrection Jesus said: "And no unclean thing can enter into his kingdom; therefore nothing entereth into his rest save it be those who have washed their garments in my blood, because of their faith, and the repentance of all their sins, and their faithfulness unto the end. Now this is the commandment: Repent all ye ends of the earth and come unto me and be baptized in my name, that ye may be sanctified by the reception of the Holy Ghost, that ye may stand spotless before me at the last day. Therefore, if ye do these things blessed are ye, for ye shall be lifted up at the last day" (2 Nephi 27: 19-20; 22).

Jesus added this instruction within His

Sermon on the Mount: "Enter ye in at the strait gate: for wide is the gate, and broad is the way, that leadeth to destruction, and many there be which go in thereat: Because strait is the gate, and narrow is the way, which leadeth unto life, and few there be that find it" (Matthew 7:13-14).

Baptism in the Name of Jesus Christ Is Required

Baptism for the remission of sins is the ordinance of the gospel that opens the strait gate and puts you on the narrow path, which leads one to heaven. Once you have been baptized and you are standing on the other side of the strait gate, then you can receive the gift of the Holy Ghost by the laying on of hands.

Jesus taught Nicodemus: "Except a man be born of water and of the Spirit he cannot enter into the kingdom of God" (John 3:5).

To our father Adam God spake directly by his own voice and told Adam what he had to do to get to heaven: "And he called upon our father Adam by his own voice, saying: I am God; I made the world, and men before they were in the flesh.

And he also said unto him: If thou wilt turn unto me, and hearken unto my voice, and believe, and repent of all thy transgressions, and be baptized, even in water, in the name of mine

Only Begotten Son, who is full of grace and truth, which is Jesus Christ, the only name which shall be given under heaven, whereby salvation shall come unto the children of men, ye shall receive the gift of the Holy Ghost, asking all things in his name, and whatsoever ye shall ask, it shall be given you" (Moses 6:51-52).

The Gift of the Holy Ghost Is Required

During his mortal ministry Jesus taught thus: "If ye love me, keep my commandments and I will pray the Father and he shall give you another Comforter, that he may abide with you for ever; Even the Spirit of truth; whom the world cannot receive, because it seeth him not, neither knoweth him: but ye know him; for he dwelleth with you, and shall be in you" (John 14: 16-17). The Savior has just described, the gift of the Holy Ghost.

Becoming Child-like Is Required

Jesus also taught us the importance of being child-like, "Suffer the little children to come unto me, and forbid them not, for of such is the kingdom of God. Verily I say unto you, whosoever shall not receive the kingdom of God as a little child, he shall not enter therein" (Mark 10:14-15).

The Most Complete Answer Given by Jesus

The most complete answer given by Jesus follows: "And when he was gone forth into the way, there came one running, and kneeled to him, and asked him, Good Master, what shall I do that I may inherit eternal life? And Jesus said unto him Why callest thou me good? There is none good but one, that is, God. Thou knowest the commandments, Do not commit adultery, Do not kill, Do not steal, Do not bear false witness, Defraud not, Honour thy father and mother. And he answered and said unto him, Master, all these have I observed from my youth. Then Jesus beholding him, loved him, and said unto him, One thing thou lackest: go thy way, sell whatsoever thou hast, and give to the poor, and thou shalt have treasure in heaven: and come, take up the cross, and follow me. And he was sad at that saying and went away grieved: for he had great possessions. And Jesus looked round about, and saith unto his disciples, How hardly shall they that have riches enter into the kingdom of God! And the disciples were astonished at his words. But Jesus answereth again, and saith unto them, Children, how hard is it for them that trust in riches to enter into the kingdom of God. It is easier for a camel to go through the eye of a needle, than for a rich man to enter into the kingdom of God" (Mark 10:17-25).

The same story in the gospel of Matthew has Jesus adding the second great commandment to his answer: "and, Thou shalt love thy neighbor as thyself" (Matthew 19: 19).

What One Should Not Do to Get to Heaven

Jesus made it very clear what we should not do to get into heaven: "For I say unto you, That except your righteousness shall exceed the righteousness of the scribes and Pharisees, ye shall in no case enter into the kingdom of heaven" (Matthew 5:20). Why were the scribes and Pharisees unrighteous? Jesus has given us the answer:

"Then spake Jesus to the multitude, and to his disciples, Saying, The scribes and the Pharisees sit at Moses' seat: All therefore whatsoever they bid you observe, that observe and do: but do not ye after their works: for they say, and do not. For they bind heavy burdens and grievous to be borne, and lay them on men's shoulders; but they themselves will not move them with one of their fingers. But all their works they do to be seen of men: they make broad their phylacteries, and enlarge the borders of their garments. And love the uppermost rooms at feasts, and the chief seats in the synagogues. And greeting in the markets, and to be called of men, Rabbi, Rabbi. But be not ye called Rabbi: for one is your Master, even Christ; and all ye are brethren. And call no man your father upon the earth: for one is you Father, which is in heaven. Neither be ye called masters, for one is your Master, even Christ. But he that is greatest among you shall be your servant. And whosoever shall exalt himself shall be abased: and he that shall humble himself shall be exalted. But woe unto you scribes and Pharisees, hypocrites! for ye shut up the kingdom of heaven against men: for ye neither go in yourselves, neither suffer ye them that are entering to go in. Woe unto you, scribes and Pharisees, hypocrites! For ye devour widows' houses, and for a pretence make long prayer: therefore ye shall receive the greater damnation. Woe unto you scribes and Pharisees, hypocrites! For ye compass sea and land to make one proselyte, and

when he is made, ye make him twofold more the child of hell than yourselves. Woe unto you blind guides, which say, Whosoever shall swear by the temple, it is nothing, but whosoever shall swear by the gold of the temple, he is a debtor!
Ye fools and blind: for whether is greater, the gold, or the temple that sanctifieth the gold? And, Whosoever shall swear by the altar, it is nothing; but whosoever sweareth by the gift that is upon it, he is guilty. Ye fools and blind: for whether is greater, the gift, or the altar that sanctifieth the gift? Whoso therefore shall swear by the altar, sweareth by it, and by all things thereon. And whoso shall swear by the temple, sweareth by it, and by him that dwelleth therin. And he that shall swear by heaven, sweareth by the throne of God, and by him that sitteth thereon. Woe unto you, scribes and Pharisees, hypocrites! For ye pay tithe of mint and anise and cumin and have omitted the weightier matters of the law, judgment, mercy and faith: these ought ye to have done, and not to leave the other undone. Ye blind guides, which strain at a gnat, and swallow a camel. Woe unto you, scribes and Pharisees, hypocrites! for ye make clean the outside of the cup and of the platter, but within they are full of extortion and excess. Thou blind Pharisee, cleanse first that which is within the cup and platter, that the outside of them may be clean also. Woe unto you scribes and Pharisees,

hypocrites! for ye are like unto whited sepulchers, which indeed appear beautiful outward, but are within full of dead men's bones, and of all uncleanness. Even so ye also outwardly appear righteous unto men, but within ye are full of hypocrisy and iniquity. Woe unto you, scribes and Pharisees, hypocrites! Because ye build the tombs of the prophets, and garnish the sepulchers of the righteous,

And say, If we had been in the days of our fathers, we would not have been partakers with them in the blood of the prophets. Wherefore ye be witnesses unto yourselves, that ye are the children of them which killed the prophets.
Fill ye up then the measure of your fathers.
Ye serpents, ye generation of vipers, how can ye escape the damnation of hell? Wherefore, behold, I send unto you prophets, and wise men, and some of them ye shall kill and crucify; and some of them ye scourge in your synagogues, and persecute them from city to city: That upon you may come all the righteous blood shed upon the earth from Abel unto the blood of Zacharias whom ye slew between the temple and the altar" (Matthew 23:1-35).

I have given you the answers Jesus has given all men in order that they might get back to heaven. If I have left anything out: loving God with all your heart; and with all your soul and with all your mind: And loving your neighbor as

What Do I Have to Do to Get to Heaven?

you love yourself, will cover you and the atonement of Jesus Christ and the grace of Christ will make up the difference. God judges all men according to their works and the desire of their hearts. Therefore, if your desire is to love God and keep his commandments and endure until the end, you shall have eternal life, which is another way of saying, you shall return to live with God in heaven forever!

How do I know? The prophet Joseph Smith was given this answer in a vision he received in the temple in Kirkland, Ohio on January 21, 1836: "Thus came the voice of the Lord unto me, saying: All who have died without a knowledge of this gospel, who would have received it if they had been permitted to tarry, shall be heirs of the celestial kingdom of God; Also all that shall die henceforth without a knowledge of it, who would have received it with all their hearts, shall be heirs of that kingdom; For I the Lord, will judge all men according to their works, according to the desire of their hearts. And I also beheld that all children who die before they arrive at the age of accountability are saved in the kingdom of heaven" (D&C 137: 7-10). Normal children reach the "age of accountability when eight years old" (D&C 68: 25).

The gospel of Jesus Christ is all about eternal families. Once you are baptized, eagerly prepare yourself to visit the temple. The sealing power found only in the Lord's holy temples opens the door to exaltation and eternal families. Yes, you can live with your family in heaven forever, following this earth life. Ask the missionaries to tell you about this.

Endure Until the End

Let us not forget that repentance is not a one-time act. Repentance is a lifetime process. We must all endure until the end. "But he that shall endure unto the end, the same shall be saved" (Matthew 23:14).

Chapter Twenty-Seven

The Gospel of Jesus Christ

If you want to understand what the pure gospel of Jesus Christ is, read the Book of Mormon. To get you started, please read on.
Following the crucifixion of Jesus Christ, our Savior was indeed resurrected and Jesus visited the American continent and the people living there to teach them about his gospel. This is what the resurrected Christ said about his gospel to the people who lived on the American

continent until 421 A.D.: "Behold I have given unto you my gospel, and this is the gospel which I have given unto you-that I came into the world to do the will of my Father, because my Father sent me. And my Father sent me that I might be lifted up upon the cross; and after that I have been lifted up upon the cross, that I might draw all men unto me, that as I have been lifted up by men even so should men be lifted up by the Father, to stand before me, to be judged of their works, whether they be good or whether they be evil-And for this cause have I been lifted up; therefore, according to the power of the Father I will draw all men unto me, that they may be judged according to their works. And it shall come to pass, that whoso repenteth and is baptized in my name shall be filled and if he endureth to the end, behold, him will I hold guiltless before my Father at that day when I shall stand to judge the world. And he that endureth not unto the end, the same is he that is also hewn down and cast into the fire, from whence they can no more return, because of the justice of the Father. And this is the word which he hath given unto the children of men. And for this cause he fulfilleth the words which he hath given, and he lieth not, but fulfilleth all his words. And no unclean thing can enter into his kingdom; therefore nothing entereth into his rest save it be those who have washed their garments in my blood, because of their faith, and the repentance of all their sins, and their faithfulness unto the end.

Now this is the commandment: Repent, all ye ends of the earth, and come unto me and be baptized in my name, that ye may be sanctified by the reception of the Holy Ghost, that ye may stand spotless before me at the last day. Verily, verily, I say unto you, this is my gospel; and ye know the things that ye must do in my church; for the works which ye have seen me do that shall ye also do; for that which ye have seen me do even that shall ye do; Therefore, if ye do these things blessed are ye, for ye shall be lifted up at the last day" (3 Nephi 27:13-22).

The Parable of Three Selfish Strangers

Three strangers stood at the gates of a fortified city under siege by the enemy and begged to be let in. The captain of the city summoned his lieutenant to open the gates and let them in. "Bring them before me," said the captain to his lieutenant. "I will hear their cause to see if it is just."

Two men and a woman stood before the captain. The captain began, "I have no food or water to give you, our own people are starving. I go to the enemy to beg them to spare the lives of our women and children while the rest of us fight the enemy with what weapons and strength we have left."

"Don't worry about us," said one of the strangers. "I have my own broth," said the woman. "And I have rice and water for myself," said another. "I also have my own food and water," said the last. "We ask only to share your shelter and protection from the enemy," said the first.

"Cast them back into the world and let them fend for themselves," said the captain to his lieutenant. "You have not understood the gospel of Jesus Christ. And in the short time you have stood before me, you have judged yourselves and you will also say that I have judged you but it is each of you who are judged of yourselves.

You have not sought to love your neighbor as thyself but you have only sought to love yourselves. You did not offer to share your food and water with us but only sought our protection and shelter from the enemy. Neither did you offer to share your weapons with us or to fight the enemy with us for your own lives."

Love Is the Heart of the Gospel

The heart and soul of the gospel of Jesus Christ is love. Man must love everything God's hands have made, judge no one and forgive everyone. That is pretty much the heart, and soul of the gospel of Jesus Christ. Before Jesus Christ walked the earth, men were taught to live by the Law of Moses. Jesus gave us a new law: "Ye have heard that it hath been said, Thou shalt love thy neighbor and hate thine enemy" (Matthew 5:43).

But Jesus did away with all that. Jesus taught that which no man's ears had ever heard before. His words must have been a powerful shock to those who first heard them: "But I say unto you. Love your enemies, bless them that curse you, do good to them that hate you, and pray for them which despitefully use you and persecute you. That ye may be the children of your Father which is in heaven: for he maketh his sun to rise on the evil and on the good, and sendeth rain on the just and on the unjust" (Matthew 5:44

Chapter Twenty-Eight

The Book of Mormon

Some time ago I had a family home evening in my home for the family I was home teaching. Following a nice dinner, we watched a movie about missionaries and snacked on popcorn and lemonade. Then everyone was going to take a turn reading one verse of the first chapter of the Book of Mormon. When we came to verse 13 of the first chapter, it was a little eight-year old girl's turn to read. I had just had the privilege of baptizing her a little earlier so she was barely eight years old. She began: "And he read, saying: Wo, wo, unto Jerusalem, for I have seen thine *abominations!* Yea, and many things did my father read concerning Jerusalem that it should be destroyed, and the inhabitants thereof; many should perish by the sword and many should be carried away captive into Babylon" (1 Nephi 1:13).

When she finished reading her verse, I asked the little girl, "What does abominations mean?" She answered me, "That's when God dropped a bomb on the nations." I said, "That's a very good answer." Now the grown-ups know what abominations means but out of the mouth of babes comes the pure and simple truth.

Are there any books out there besides the Bible and the Book of Mormon that teach us about God the Eternal Father, and Jesus Christ?

Yes. Besides the Bible and the Book of Mormon our beloved Father in heaven has given us the Doctrine and Covenants and the Pearl of Great Price to teach us about God and Christ and to reveal to us the fullness of the gospel of Jesus Christ.

Are there any world famous works of literature that teach us about God the Father and Jesus Christ? Many books allude to the existence of God and many books use any number of metaphors to allude to Christ.

I found Dale Carnegie quoting one of my favorite scriptures in his book, *How To Win Friends and Influence People.* He included, "For inasmuch as ye have done it unto one of the least of thy brethren, ye have done it unto me." It would have been even better if he had included the scriptural reference so that readers uncertain as to where those words came from would know they came from God. (See, Matthew 25:40).

To my knowledge, there is but one author and one book only; that uses both the name of Christ and quotes scripture from the Bible giving the scriptural reference. That book is, "The Brothers Karamazov by Fyodor Dostoyevsky. Dostoyevsky gives us the following conversation between a monk and Father Ferapont:

"Do you see this tree?" asked Father Ferapont, after a pause.

"I do, blessed Father."

"You think it's an elm, but for me it has another shape."

"What sort of shape?" Inquired the monk, after a pause of vain expectation.

"It happens at night. You see those two branches? In the night it is Christ holding out His arms to me and seeking me with those arms, I see it clearly and tremble. It's terrible. terrible!"

"What is there terrible if it's Christ Himself?"

"Why, He'll snatch me up and carry me away."

"Alive?"

"In the spirit and glory of Elijah, haven't you heard? He will take me in His arms and bear me away." (From the Brothers Karamozov by Fyodor Dostoyevsky, p. 201, Copyright 1950, Random House, Inc).

The Book of Mormon

The following scripture not only made its way into the text of the Brothers Karamozov, it is also carved into Dostoyevsky's tombstone. (From Wikipedia, Joseph Frank biographer: 1979 pp.6-22; Kesla biographer: 1989, pp. 1-6).

"Verily, verily, I say unto you, Except a corn fall into the ground and die, it abideth alone: but if it die, it bringeth forth much fruit" (John 12:24).

There is a very good reason for Dostoyevsky quoting the New Testament of the Bible in his writings. Dostoyevsky spent eight years in one of the harshest and most cruel prisons in Russia when he was a young man and all he had to read was a copy of the New Testament of the Bible. (From Wikipedia, The Free Encyclopedia).

What translation of the New Testament was Dostoyevsky reading? I do not know. I was not there with him when he was reading it. But the words to the verses he quotes match the words to the same verses found in my King James translation of the New Testament perfectly.

The Book of Mormon is the most perfect book every written. Why? Because it was written by prophets of God who were inspired by the promptings of the Holy Ghost to write only what God the Eternal Father would have them write. The Book of Mormon was translated from Reformed Egyptian (a forgotten language) into English-by Joseph Smith who God called to be

His prophet to usher in this last dispensation of times. Remember, "all tings are written by the Father" (3 Nephi 27: 26). "Surely the Lord God will do nothing but he reveleth his secret unto his servants, the prophets" (Amos 3:7).

A prophet of God is a servant of God who is called of God and ordained of God and given the authority of God to speak the words God would have him speak and to write the words God would have him write.

If Moses did not speak and write the word of God we would not have the beginning of the Old Testament including the books of Genesis, Exodus, Leviticus, Numbers and Deuteronomy.

We would not have a record of Moses living in Egypt for forty years and Moses wandering with his people in the wilderness for another forty years. We would have no record of God's ten commandments. We would have no knowledge of the Law of Moses.

There would be no record of Moses calling upon Almighty God to bring plagues and torments upon the Pharaoh of Egypt, which would eventually allow Moses to take his people out of Egypt. We would have no record of Moses parting the Red Sea and allowing his people to cross the Red Sea onto dry land.

If father Lehi did not hearken unto the voice of God and take his family out of Jerusalem when God told him to leave that place, he and all

The Book of Mormon

his family would have perished there.

But more importantly, if father Lehi did not follow the instructions of God and cause his sons to go back to Jerusalem "three times" after they had fled into the wilderness and recover the sacred records of God, and continue to write what God revealed to him (his prophet), we would not have the Book of Mormon today. If father Lehi and all the prophets that followed him did not continue to write down the words of God and the events that would cause men to believe there was a God, we would not have those words and testimonies and faith promoting stories in the Book of Mormon today.

The Book of Mormon was written by the hand of God and was given by the inspiration of the Holy Ghost to many prophets of God from 600 B.C. until 421 A.D. one word at a time and one line at a time until the record was complete in the eyes of God. The Book of Mormon was originally written in Reformed Egyptian to save space writing on Brass and Gold plates that would endure the elements of wear and tear through the ages. The Book of Mormon record was given to Joseph Smith in 1820. The prophet Moroni finished his work on the earth around 421 A.D. but returned to the earth as an angel of God in 1820 and took young Joseph Smith to the place where the Book of Mormon record had been deposited.

The Book of Mormon is available for all to read today. The Book of Mormon contains the fullness of the gospel of Jesus Christ. The Book of Mormon is another witness and testimony of Jesus Christ. Joseph Smith said of the Book of Mormon: "It is the keystone of our religion and a man could draw nearer to God by reading it than by reading any other book." "The Book of Mormon has been translated in its entirety into 92 languages. As of March 2015 the Church of Jesus Christ of Latter-day Saints continues to publish at least portions of the Book of Mormon in 110 languages" (From Wikipedia).

We have this record from the new testament of the King James translation of the Bible, which foretells the Savior's visit: to his other sheep on the American continent. These other sheep spoken of were the Book of Mormon people. From the gospel of John we read:

"As the Father knoweth me, even so know I the Father: and I lay down my life for the sheep. And other sheep I have, which are not of this fold: them also I must bring, and they shall hear my voice; and there shall be one fold, and one shepherd. Therefore doth my Father love me, because I lay down my life, that I might take it again. No man taketh it from me, but I lay it down of myself. I have power to lay it down, and I have power to take it again. This commandment have I received of my Father" (John 10:15-18).

The resurrected Christ did indeed visit those people who survived the destruction of that part of the world (in the Americas) following his crucifixion and resurrection. The resurrected Jesus stood in front of all those people and allowed each one to handle him and see and touch and feel the wounds in his hands and feet and side.

"And it came to pass that the Lord spake unto them saying: Arise and come forth unto me, that ye may thrust your hands into my side, and also that ye may feel the prints of the nails in my hands and in my feet, that ye may know that I am the God of Israel, and the God of the whole earth, and have been slain for the sins of the world.

And it came to pass that the multitude went forth, and thrust their hands into his side, and did feel the prints of the nails in his hands and in his feet; and this they did do, going forth one by one until they had all gone forth, and did see with their eyes and did feel with their hands, and did know of a surety and did bear record, that it was he, of whom it was written by the prophets, that should come" (3 Nephi 11:13-14).

Does that sound familiar?

"And when they had all gone forth and had witnessed for themselves, they did cry out with one accord, saying: Hosanna! Blessed be the name of the Most High God! And they did fall down at the feet of Jesus and did worship him" (3 Nephi 11:16-17).

A similar scene unfolded in the old world following the resurrection of our Savior. The resurrected Christ spoke these words to the remaining apostles living near Jerusalem following his resurrection when he appeared to those men living there: "Handle me and see for a spirit hath not flesh and bones as ye see me have" (Luke 24:39).

Chapter Twenty-Nine

Faith in Jesus Christ Changes Lives

The following report comes from a returned missionary who left our home ward to serve his mission. He has given me permission to share his story:

"About two years ago, I stood here before you and I told you why I thought faith in Jesus Christ would change lives. I'm afraid at that time I didn't quite know what I was talking about. I feared a lot when I stood before you. But today, I stand here with confidence to tell you that faith in Jesus Christ changes lives. It has changed my life and it has changed the people I taught and the people that have come before me.

What is faith? The Bible says that: "faith is the substance of things hoped for, the evidence of things not seen" (Hebrews 11:1). The Book of

Mormon, prophet Alma went on to say, "and now as I said concerning faith-faith is not to have a perfect knowledge of things; therefore if you have faith you hope for things which are not seen, which are true" (Alma 32:21). So if you were my investigator in West Africa in Ghana, I might say, "Do you believe in Jesus Christ?" And hopefully, you would say, "yes." Then I would say, "Did you ever see Jesus Christ?" And you would say, "oh, no." Then I would ask again, "Do you have faith in Jesus Christ," and you would say, "yes." Then I would say, "Wait, not quite yet." Because; the General Epistle of James tells us that "faith without works is dead" (James 2:20). So faith is a principle of action. If you have faith, you must act. For all those that I taught on my mission in Ghana, that was the key factor, if they truly had faith, they acted. How can we increase our faith in Jesus Christ?

  It is easy to have faith in many things. I have faith that my mom will help me with many things. Many of us have faith the sun will rise-or our car will start. But it is a little more difficult to have faith in Jesus Christ and it is something that was really hard for me to understand for a long time. Well how do we do it, how do we find our faith in him, in Jesus Christ? First, we have to learn about him. You have to hear the words of Christ. And the words of Christ will teach you all things.

Faith in Jesus Christ Changes Lives

The Book of Alma teaches us in chapter 32, verse 28, "Now, we will compare the word unto a seed. Now, if ye give place, that a seed may be planted in your heart, behold, if it be a true seed, or a good seed, if ye do not cast it out by your unbelief, that ye will resist the Spirit of the Lord, behold, it will begin to swell within your breasts; and when you feel these swelling motions, ye will begin to say within yourselves-It must needs be that this is a good seed, or that the word is good, for it beginneth to enlarge my soul; yea, it beginneth to enlighten my understanding, yea, it beginneth to be delicious to me" (Alma 32:28). The enlightenment of your understanding will come. When I went on a mission, I heeded the call. I took that word that the prophet had said to serve a mission and I wanted to test it. I wanted to see if that seed would grow so I planted it in my heart and I acted and the results were amazing. The results were more than I could have ever expected. I had heard the Joseph Smith story so many times. I had heard that Jesus was the Christ.

But it wasn't until I was sitting under a Mango tree in the middle of West Africa, after I had thrown up a few times after eating food I had never even imagined was possible. I remember listening to my trainer teach: Jesus Christ established a church. But that church fell.

Change Your Life Forever

There was an apostasy. But there was now a need for a restoration, a restitution of all things. And I thought to myself, wow! Jesus Christ really did establish a church. There really was an apostasy. Joseph Smith really was a prophet. But it wasn't until I had acted that my understanding was enlightened just like the Book of Mormon said. It wasn't until I had gone through trials that that testimony was able to come. And I am so grateful. But fortunately for me, I wasn't the only convert on my mission. I needed to be converted before I could teach others. But I have seen so many people change their lives through their faith in Jesus Christ.

One person who I remember well was a woman named Christa Bell Cabell. There was one hot and sweaty day, we were teaching an investigator and the lesson wasn't moving, it wasn't going anywhere. I remember sitting in that lesson praying, "Heavenly Father why do you want us to be teaching this person at this time?" I looked over and I saw a house that I had never seen before. I thought to myself, "we need to go to that house."

The person at the door said, "I'm not interested, but maybe, my sister might be interested. Soon, a girl came to the door and she introduced herself as Crista Bell. I thought, "She doesn't really speak English. It is really hard to understand her." And as we walked away from that lesson, I thought to myself, "How could that have been a prompting?" We're out here looking for the elect, someone who could be a bishop or a relief society president, and you just gave me someone who doesn't speak English. Well, I was wrong. I was so, so wrong. Because it wasn't until church that Sunday, when the door opened and in came this scarred little 19 year-old girl. I said to my companion, "That's the girl that didn't speak English and she's at church." All those other people with great big houses we were contacting didn't come but the girl who didn't speak English was there. She had done what she needed to do. She had followed the promptings of the Holy Ghost without much of our help and she was there. After church we took her into the bishop's office. We had a great bishop who loved to meet the investigators on their first day. The bishop asked her, "Christa Bell, how was church?" She answered in English with a sincere testimony, "God is here." And the spirit filled that room so fast. The girl who could barely speak English just testified to us that God was there, that God was in that building. And Crista Bell acted. She continued to act. She took that testimony she felt and she didn't stop. I remember when we would come to church she would already be there taking hymn books and putting them on the chairs. And it was because of that faith that her life changed.

She continued. When I was transferred, it was hard to say goodbye. But that girl that didn't speak English would call me and she would read scriptures over the phone to me and I remember the day that she asked me, "Can you help me to understand, "Helaman, chapter Five verse 12? "And now my sons, remember, remember." She said, "Elder can you help me understand what that means?" I thought to myself, wait you can barely speak English, wait, you can read? But I forgot, that faith in Jesus Christ changes lives. And she helped to build my testimony, that faith in Jesus Christ changes lives, all of our lives, if we put our faith in him. And through the atonement of Jesus Christ all of our lives can be changed.

Another such person was a woman named Vita Johnnie. We met her on a cloudy day; it was about to rain. I can remember saying to my companion, "We've got to hurry and find someone that will let us into their house before the rain comes." It was one of the few times we were let into someone's home. Most of our lessons were taught outside. We met this girl named Vita, she was like a vitamin; she helped people. So we met Vita and we sat down. We asked her, "Vita, what do you want most in life?" She said, "I really want to go to heaven."

I thought great, we can help you get there, and we taught her the gospel of Jesus

Faith in Jesus Christ Changes Lives

Christ. What is the gospel of Jesus Christ? The first principles are: faith, repentance, baptism; receiving the Holy Ghost, enduring to the end. And that seed, that word of faith that was planted in her, did not stop growing. She was another person who continued to act and to act again, over and over. She was an average person when we met her. But I remember walking into the temple with her for her endowment when she was wearing white thinking, "Wow, faith in Jesus Christ changes lives!" She too would send me scriptures every Sunday trying to strengthen me and she did strengthen me. I remember, it was after a trip to the temple, that she told me, "Elder, I am going to serve a mission." I wasn't sure if I believed her or not. Well, she ended up serving in the same zone as me on the last month of my mission. And it was amazing to see someone you had just met on the street as an average person, testify to a group of missionaries that Jesus Christ is real, that Joseph Smith was a prophet and that faith in Jesus Christ changes lives.

And it was through her and through my own experiences that I learned that. And it was amazing to see those people change. The people of Ghana are so humble. And it allowed me and other people to see how their faith in Jesus Christ could change their lives. Sometimes, we would see all the problems there. We would see all the poverty and we would think, if only I could get a thousand dollars and get it over here and then I could help someone. Then we would say, "wait, that's not what they need. They need the gospel of Jesus Christ. It's the only thing that can change them. It's the only thing that can help them to grow and to strengthen themselves both: physically, mentally, spiritually and in education."

But all of those people face challenges. Crista Bell's stepmother stabbed her with a knife because she went to church. For Vita, when we showed up to her baptism, we had filled the font the night before. When we came back the next day, the water was gone and we cancelled the baptism. The next week, the same thing happened and we had to drive about ten kilometers to get to another church where she was finally baptized in about a foot of water. But remember what Moroni told us: It is only after the trial of your faith that you receive a witness and a testimony that your life will be changed. (See Ether 12:6).

And always remember that when Jesus Christ brings you a message, when those with the truth come, Satan will come also. If I could just start to number the rumors that are in Ghana about what we do in the temple or what we do in the Church, I could go on and on, things you would never think of. But in the Book of

Faith in Jesus Christ Changes Lives

Helaman, he reminds us that Satan goes around spreading rumors and lies, to deceive you, to harden the hearts of the people. And I would say that many of our hearts are hardened. Many people got hardened there because of those rumors. But remember, if you know someone who's heart is hardened, it isn't only their faith alone that will change their life. When the angel appeared to Alma the Younger, he told him, "It is because of the faith and the prayers of your father and family that I am here." And I believe that if we find those people who are struggling, whose hearts are hardened, that if we pray and if we are patient, if we wait on the prodigal, their lives will be changed just like all of those Book of Mormon stories.

If you are lost, I encourage you to focus a lot less on the stories you have heard and a lot more on the outcome. I encourage you to look at the people who really live the gospel. Not the people who put on a face, not the people who come to church every day, but the people who put the gospel in their homes. I encourage you to look at them and ask yourself, "Where did that come from?" And you will find it came from the gospel of Jesus Christ and it is because of the atonement of Jesus Christ. Moroni told us that every good thing comes from God. Every thing which inviteth and enticeth to do good, and to love God, and to serve him, is inspired of God" (Moroni 7:14).

And I know that the gospel of Jesus Christ and the Church of Jesus Christ of Latter-day Saints comes from God. I know that the gospel of Jesus Christ is real. I know that when we are obedient to the commandments, it will always bring us blessings. And when we are not, it will always bring a loss of blessings. I know that the Book of Mormon is real and it is true because I have read it and I have tested it and I have put it before people and I have seen them change their lives because of it. I know that Joseph Smith was a prophet, not because I knew him or even because I believe his story but because I have seen the fruits of his labors and the fruits of his calling. Because I have seen that which God has called him to do, has resulted in wonderful things.

But the most important thing that I learned on my mission and I will probably ever learn is that Jesus Christ is the Savior, and that it is only through him that we can come to heaven to enter into the celestial kingdom and to be together again, is through faith on him. There shall be no other way or means whereby salvation can come unto the children of men, only in and through Christ, the Lord Omnipotent. (See Mosiah 3:18). I know that he is real and I know that I will serve him until I die and that each of us should do likewise. I leave you these things in the name of Jesus Christ. Amen."

A note to the reader from the author: I have listened to hundreds upon hundreds of talks from returned missionaries in my lifetime. This is the "creme de la creme." The best, of the best. The young man who has given this talk has carefully outlined what one must do to change your life for the better forever. If you will follow what he has outlined, if you will put his words into action and prove that you have faith to believe in his words, which are the words of Christ repeated to you, you will indeed be able to change your life for the better forever!

I am proud of all of our young men and women who honor our beloved Savior by serving their missions in 150 different countries of the world. They are a constant inspiration to me. May God continue to bless and protect all of you as you teach all the sons and daughters of God throughout the world the precious and magnificent, life changing; gospel of Jesus Christ.

Chapter Thirty

How to Tell If You Have Found the True Church of Jesus Christ

Here are just a few things for you to check to see if you have found the true Church of Jesus Christ:

The True Church of Jesus Christ Must Be Called: The Church of Jesus Christ

Jesus set down the requirements for all to follow who would be a part of his Church when he visited the Nephite Saints in the new world, following his crucifixion and resurrection. The Lord said: "Therefore, whatsoever ye shall do, ye shall do it in my name; therefore ye shall call the church in my name; and ye shall call upon the Father in my name that he will bless the church for my sake. And how be it my church save it be called in my name? For if a church be called in Moses' name then it be Moses' church; or if it be called in the name of a man then it be the church of a man; but if it be called in my name then it is my church," (3 Nephi 27:7-8).

The True Church of Jesus Christ Must Be Built Upon the Gospel of Jesus Christ

Jesus continued to explain what is required to have part in his true Church. "But if it (the Church) be called in my name then it is my church, if it so be that they are built upon my gospel. Verily I say unto you, that ye are built upon my gospel; therefore ye shall call whatsoever things ye do call, in my name; therefore if ye call upon the Father, for the church, if it be in my name the Father will hear you; and if it so be that the church is built upon my gospel then will the Father show forth his own works in it. But if it be not built upon my gospel, and is built upon the works of men, or upon the works of the devil, verily I say unto you they have joy in their works for a season, and by and by the end cometh, and they are hewn down and cast into the fire, from whence there is no return. For their works do follow them, for it is because of their works that they are hew down; therefore remember the thing that I have told you" (3 Nephi 27:8-12).

The True Church of Jesus Christ Must Be Built Upon A Foundation of Apostles and Prophets

Why? Because that is the way Jesus built his church while he was on the earth. The apostle Paul taught, "Now therefore ye are no more strangers and foreigners, but fellow citizens with the saints, and of the household of God: And are built upon a foundation of apostles and prophets, Jesus Christ himself being the chief corner stone" (Ephesians 2:19-20).

The True Church of Jesus Christ Must Have Priesthood Authority to Act in God's Name

When Jesus organized his Church during his mortal ministry in the old world, he called his twelve apostles forth and ordained them and gave them power to act in his name. From the gospel according to Mark we read, "And he ordained twelve, that they should be with him, and that he might send them forth to preach, And to have power to heal sicknesses and to cast out devils" (Mark 5:14-15). The account from Matthew adds to this, "And when he had called unto him his twelve disciples, he gave them power against unclean spirits, to cast them out, and to heal all manner of sickness and all manner of disease. Now the names of the twelve apostles are these; The first, Simon, who is called Peter, and Andrew his brother; James the son of Zebedee and John his brother; Phillip, and Bartholomew; Thomas, and Matthew the publican; James, the son of Alphaeus, and Lebbaeus, who's surname is Thaddaeus; Simon the Canaanite, and Judas Iscariot, who also betrayed him. These twelve Jesus sent forth, and commanded them, saying, Go not into the way of the Gentiles, and into any city of the Samaritans enter ye not: But go rather to the lost sheep of the house of Israel. And as ye go, preach, saying, the kingdom of heaven is at hand. Heal the sick, cleanse the lepers, raise the dead, cast out devils: freely ye have received, freely give" (Matthew 10:1-8).

The True Church of Jesus Christ Must Have No Paid Ministry

When Jesus called forth and ordained his twelve apostles he charged them, "Provide neither gold, nor silver, nor brass in your purses. Nor scrip for your journey, neither two coats, neither shoes, nor yet staves: for the workman is worthy of his meat" (Matthew 10:9-10).

The True Church of Jesus Christ Must Be a Missionary Church

Why? Because Jesus sent out missionaries when he was on the earth to every nation, kindred; tongue and people. We read from the scripture: "Go ye therefore and teach all nations, baptizing them in the name of the Father, and of the Son, and of the Holy Ghost: Teaching them to observe all things whatsoever I have commanded you: and, lo, I am with you alway, even until the end of the world. Amen" (Matthew 28:19-20).

The True Church of Jesus Christ Must Build Temples

Why? Because: Jesus visited the temple during his mortal ministry. When Jesus was but a babe, Simeon looked upon the babe in the temple and declared, "mine eyes have seen thy salvation" (Luke 2:30). And Anna also "coming in that same instant gave thanks likewise unto the Lord, and spake of him to all them that looked for redemption in Jerusalem" (Luke 2 38). Jesus taught the doctors of the law in the temple when he was a boy. (Luke 5:17). Later, Jesus cast out the moneychangers from the temple grounds. (Matthew 21:12). We read that in those days Jesus was daily in the temple. (Luke 19:47; Luke 22:53). Sacred priesthood ordinances were performed in the temple. The apostle Paul said:

"Else what shall they do that are baptized for the dead, if the dead rise not at all? Why are they then baptized for the dead" (1 Corinthians 15:29)? (Luke 2:25-40). Anna was four score and four years or 84 years old. She departed not from the temple but served God with fastings and prayers night and day" (Luke 2:37).

The True Church of Jesus Christ Must Practice the Law of the Fast

The priestess, Anna fasted in the temple both night and day as we have just read. Jesus fasted for forty days and forty nights during his ministry after which he was tempted of the devil. When Jesus walked the earth, the Law of the Fast was already in practice. The prophet Isaiah has given us the law of the fast in his writings. Said he, "Is it such a fast that I have chosen? A day for a man to afflict his soul? Is it to bow down his head as a bulrush, and to spread sackcloth and ashes under him? Wilt thou call this a fast, and an acceptable day unto the Lord? Is not this the fast that I have chosen? To loose the bands of wickedness, to undo the heavy burdens, and to

How to Tell If You Have Found the True Church of Jesus Christ

let the oppressed go free, and that ye break every yoke? Is it not to deal thy bread to the hungry, and that thou bring the poor that are cast out to thy house? When thou seest the naked, that thou cover him, and that thou hide not thyself from thine own flesh? Then shall thy light break forth as the morning, and thy health shall spring forth speedily: and thy righteousness shall go before thee; the glory of the Lord shall be thy rearward. Then thou shalt call, and the Lord shall answer; thou shalt cry and he shall say, Here I am. If thou take away from the midst of thee the yoke, the putting forth of the finger, and speaking vanity; and if thou draw out thy soul to the hungry, and satisfy the afflicted soul; then shall thy light rise in obscurity, and thy darkness be as the noonday: And the Lord shall guide thee continually, and satisfy thy soul in drought, and make fat thy bones: and thou shalt be like a watered garden, and like a spring of water, whose waters fail not. And they that shall be of thee shall build the old waste places: thou shalt raise up the foundations of many generations; and thou shalt be called, The repairer of the breach, The restorer of paths to dwell in" (Isaiah 58:5-12).

The True Church of Jesus Christ Must Remember the Sabbath Day and Keep It Holy

From the Ten Commandments we read, "Remember the Sabbath day, to keep it holy. Six days shalt thou labor and do all thy work: But the Sabbath of the Lord thy God: in it thou shalt not do any work, thou, nor thy son, nor thy daughter, thy manservant, nor thy maidservant, nor thy cattle, nor thy stranger that is within thy gates: For in six days the Lord made heaven and earth, the sea, and all that in them is, and rested the seventh day: wherefore the Lord blessed the Sabbath day, and hallowed it" (Exodus 20: 8-11). The prophet Isaiah has explained how the Lord would have us worship him on the Sabbath day, "If thou turn away thy foot from the Sabbath, from doing thy pleasure on my holy day: and call the Sabbath a delight, the holy of the Lord, honourable; and shall honour him, not doing thine own ways, finding thine own pleasure, speaking thine own words: Then shall thou delight thyself in the Lord; and I will cause thee to ride upon the high places of the earth, and feed thee with the heritage of Jacob thy father:

for the mouth of the Lord hath spoken it" (Isaiah 58:13-14).

The True Church of Jesus Christ Must Live the Law of Tithing

The prophet Malachi gave us the law of tithing. We read, "Will a man rob God? Yet ye have robbed me. But ye say, Wherein have we robbed thee? In tithes and offerings. Ye are cursed with a curse: for ye have robbed me, even this whole nation. Bring ye all the tithes to the storehouse, that there may be meat in mine house, and prove me now herewith, saith the Lord of hosts, if I will not open you the windows of heaven, and pour you out a blessing, that there shall not be room enough to receive it. And I will rebuke the devourer for your sakes, and he shall not destroy the fruits of your ground; neither shall your vine cast her fruit before the time in the field, saith the Lord of hosts. And all nations shall call you blessed: for ye shall be a delightsome land, saith the Lord of hosts" (Malachi 3: 8-12).

The True Church of Jesus Christ Must Practice the First Great Commandment

"Then one of them, which was a lawyer, asked him a question, tempting him, saying, Master, which is the great commandment in the law? Jesus said unto him, Thou shalt love the Lord thy God with all thy heart, and with all thy soul, and with all thy mind. This is the first and great commandment"(Matthew 22:35-38).

The True Church of Jesus Christ Must Practice the Second Great Commandment

"And the second is like unto it, thou shalt love thy neighbor as thyself. On these two commandments hang all the law and the prophets" (Matthew 12:39-40).

The Church of Jesus Christ of Latter-day Saints today, qualifies as practicing all twelve of these requirements. But the Church of Jesus

How to Tell If You Have Found the True Church of Jesus Christ

Christ today has so much more to offer you. Seek the missionaries near you to tell you about: The Relief Society, Deacons Quorums, Teachers Quorums, Priests Quorums, Elders Quorums, High Priests Quorums, Summer Camp for Young Women, Summer Camp for Young Men. Then there is Primary, B-Hives for little girls every Sunday, and My Maids, Laurels and Young Women. Ask about the Word of Wisdom, Home Teaching and Visiting Teaching, Family Home Evening, Family Scripture Study, Family Prayer, researching your ancestors which is Genealogy, Family History Centers, Family Search.com; Temple ordinance work for our ancestors who have passed away, fast offerings, contributing to the building fund, the Book of Mormon program, the Missionary fund. Then there is the Church Welfare Program, The Bishop's storehouse, food storage and putting a little money aside for a rainy day, and Deseret Industries. The recent Proclamation on Family by the First Presidency of the Church and the Quorum of Twelve Apostles, The Mormon Tabernacle Choir, The KSL radiobroadcast every Sunday morning.

    Then we have the Church magazines: The Improvement Era, The Liahona and the Ensign. There is also the Church News, the Church website, Mormon.org. Ask the missionaries to tell you all about the Hill Cumorah Pageant in New York every summer and the Visitor's Center in Salt Lake City and in New York. Ask the missionaries to tell you all about Brigham Young University, Provo, and Brigham Young University in Rexburg Idaho and in Hawaii and New Zealand. Then there is: the seminary program and institute classes. Ask the missionaries to tell you about the Polynesian Cultural Center in Hawaii and the need for Senior missionary couples to serve in a myriad of capacities all over the world, and yes, at their own expense just like the young full-time missionaries. And there is still more for you to learn about, and all of this is available to you right now.

Chapter Thirty-One

An Invitation to Come Unto Christ

Jesus is always standing at our proverbial front door and knocking and waiting patiently for us to hear and then open the door and let him in. John the Revelator has given us the Master's invitation to all: "Behold, I stand at the door, and knock: If any man hear my voice, and open the door, I will come in to him, and will sup with him, and he with me" (Revelation 3:20).

Our beloved Savior does not care if we are red or yellow or black or white in color. Christ judges all men by their hearts and not by their outward appearance. Jesus will take you as you are and wherever you are in your eternal progression. All you have to do is pray to the Father and ask Christ to come into your life.

"And all things, whatsoever ye shall ask in prayer, believing, ye shall receive" (Matthew 21:22).

Change Your Life Forever

You Are Cordially Invited to Come Unto Christ

RSVP
BY CALLING

(888) 537-7700 within the United States
or 1-(888) 537-7700 when outside of the United States
or Go to mormon.org
and click on chat.

You may request a free copy of the Book of Mormon or the King James Version of the Bible or you may even request missionary lessons over the phone. Thank you.

An Invitation to Come Unto Christ

Here then are two of the most timely and important questions you will ever be asked to answer: Will you hear Christ knocking on the door of your heart? Will you let Jesus Christ into your life? How do you come unto Christ? "If any man hear my voice, and open the door" (Rev. 3:20). You must take the first step. God waits on man to open the door of his heart and let him in. Draw near unto me, and I will draw near unto you. (see James 4:8). God waits on man to draw near unto him.

How do I do that? The answer is clear: You must ask God the Eternal Father in the name of Christ whatsoever you may. And if you ask with faith in Christ, God will answer your prayer. When was the last time you prayed a simple, sincere and humble prayer to God? Isn't it about time for you to get back down on your knees and speak to the Father of us all?

Prayer and reading the word of God, go together like apple pie and vanilla ice cream. When you study the word of God, the Holy Ghost will inspire you with insights to the deeper meaning of God's word. Remember, the things of God are spiritual and they must be spiritually discerned. I challenge you to get started. Decide to pray. Decide to read God's word. Decide to know the truth. The truth will draw you to God then God can change your heart

Chapter Thirty-Two

Take the Missionary Lessons

"There were 85,150 missionaries serving full-time missions in 150 countries of the world in 2015 for the Church of Jesus Christ of Latter-day Saints. As of July 2015 there are 417 missions throughout the world." (From: The Missionary Department, The Church of Jesus Christ of Latter-day Saints, © by Intellectual Reserve, Inc.). The young men and women serving as missionaries who must be worthy and at least 18 and 19 years old, respectively, are paying their own way to share a message of great importance! Their message has the power to change human lives for the better forever. Their message is plain and simple: The fullness of the pure and true gospel of Jesus Christ has been restored to the earth.

Now is the time to accept the invitation given to every nation, kindred, tongue and people by our beloved Savior, Jesus Christ: "Come unto me all ye that labor and are heavy laden and I will give you rest. Take my yoke upon you, and learn of me; for I am meek and lowly in heart: and ye shall find rest to your souls" (Matthew 11:28-29).

Before you will ever be able to hear the voice of the Lord, you will have to learn how to listen. To listen correctly you must be quiet. Go find a quiet and peaceful place. You will never hear the still small voice of God if you have interfering thoughts and noises and sounds running through your head. Clear your mind of all exterior thoughts. If there is a song running through your head, wait until the song stops. Find a quiet place. Get away from all distractions. Stop. Be still and wait to hear the still small voice of the Holy Ghost.

When you can hear your own thoughts clearly, get down on your knees and ask God to tell you in His own way that He lives and loves you and that He would have you become a part of the restored gospel of Jesus Christ. When you hear the still small voice of the Spirit of God in your mind and in your heart, go and do what it prompts you to do.

These words were enough for a fourteen-year old farm boy named Joseph Smith to find a quiet place and to pray to God: "If any of you lack wisdom, let him ask of God, that giveth to all men liberally, and upbraideth not, and it shall be given unto him" (James 1:15).

These words were enough for another fourteen-year old boy named brother Guo to ask God to speak to him: "And whatsoever ye shall ask the Father in my name, which is right, believing that ye shall receive, behold, it shall be given unto you" (3 Nephi 18:20). And because he did pray and ask God, Elder Guo who's home is in Beijing. China served a full-time mission in Utah.

Take the missionary lessons. The missionary lessons will take three weeks. But as you have read in Chapter Two, the missionary lessons can be given in just one day. Take three weeks out of your earthly life to insure that your life on earth will be one filled with peace. Take three weeks to assure yourself that you might enjoy everlasting life when your work on earth is finished.

Chapter Thirty-Three

Online Missionaries

Many reading this will not know that it is possible to simply make a phone call from anywhere in the world and reach a missionary from the Church of Jesus Christ of Latter-day Saints on the other end. Because of their calling as, "Online Missionaries, they have the opportunity to pick up the phone and field incoming calls from all over the United States and the world. The call is toll free and so you now have the luxury of learning about the gospel of Jesus Christ without even leaving your home.

You may also reach the "Online Missionaries" by going to mormon.org. Once you access mormon.org, simply click on "chat, speak to a representative." The online missionaries are often able to teach the gospel to those who call and ask questions. Many of those who call join the Church of Jesus Christ of Latter-day Saints and are baptized.

Here are the phone numbers to call once again:

Within the United States call: 866-277-7700

Outside of the United States you may call: 1-866-277-7700. The calls are toll-free.

You may also access the Online Missionaries by going to: mormon.org. Then click on, speak to a representative.

You may request a free copy of The Bible and The Book of Mormon. You may also request missionaries to visit you.

Stories from Online Missionaries

The following stories were shared by our local Online Missionaries; now serving in Provo, Utah:

From Kenya to Ghana

We first came into contact with Sarah (name has been changed) in November of 2016. She was from Kenya originally, but moved to Ghana, Africa, attending Ashesi University, to study electrical engineering. She came onto Mormon.org chat, to find out more about our faith. She had seen YouTube Stars online, who were members of The Church of Jesus Christ of Latter-day Saints, and got interested in our faith. She wanted to learn more about the gift of tongues, how to worship, and why God allows bad things to happen to those who give their lives to Christ. Elder Buckway and I (Elder Withers) asked her if she would like to learn more from online missionaries, and she said that she would love that. My companion and I got her email and began teaching her through,

Google hangouts chat. She was Pentecostal before, but found that she still had so many questions. When we talked to her, she realized all of her questions were being answered. We taught her for many weeks, and helped her understand the tenets of the gospel. We catered the teaching to suit her needs, and always helped her in the way that the Spirit of the Lord directed us to. She had such great faith in God, and had such a huge desire to follow Him and do what was right. Every time we talked about one of God's commandments, she immediately started following it, and would tell us of the blessings that she saw from it. Our meetings using the internet, lasted for an hour or so, and were about twice a week. We had to work around her time zone, so that we could talk to her at a good time in her country. She lived in Ghana, Africa and we were serving our missions in Provo, Utah.

    She attended church in her area, and loved it. She met with the missionaries in Ghana, as well as meeting with us until she was baptized in January of 2017. Following her baptism, we continued to talk to her online, and she continues to also meet with the local missionaries. Her faith in God has grown immensely and her life has improved immeasurably since she found the gospel of Jesus Christ. We continue talking to her to this day.

The preceding story is from Elder Withers pictured.

The young woman Elder Withers was able to teach has sent him her conversion story in her own words. Here it is: My name is Sarah, (name has been changed). I am from Kenya, Africa and I study Electrical Engineering, at Ashesi University in Ghana. I am the second born in a family of four children. My dad is a teacher and my mom is a farmer. My home is in the mountains, a place that is so cold almost throughout the year. I grew up in the countryside until it was time for high school when I left for the city.

A very sad incident of my very close friend almost drowning and losing his life not only gave me sorrow, but also got me thinking of how truly unpredictable life is. In this sad moment, I often found myself evaluating my relationship with God. I felt that I needed to establish a more personal and close relationship with Christ and get to know more about God. Though I did not know much, I certainly knew that I wanted to live with God after death. I started attending church more frequently and bought my own Bible and started reading it.

    Despite converting to be a Protestant and actively joining, the Christian Union in school, I still had so many questions unanswered. I discovered that I knew very little about where I came from and what my purpose here on earth was. I was literally confused about what the truth is about the Christian faith and conversely, what is false about it. This was in my early teenage life: when I was trying to identify myself, and trying to gain some self-confidence. When I came to West Africa, I lost motivation of going to church because I still had the emptiness in me. I questioned many things and was uncertain concerning the choice I was to make about my spirituality.

    One day, I watched the testimony of my favorite artists', Lindsey Sterling and James the Mormon. I felt like they had a special encounter with God that I had not personally encountered and I got inspired to learn more about the Church of Jesus Christ of Latter-day Saints. The message of restoration of the gospel is the one that touched me most. It kept lingering in my head and the more I prayed about it, the more I thought about it. After a month, I decided to learn more. I started a simple online conversation with Elder Buckway and Elder Withers from Utah. Since then till my baptism into the Church of Jesus Christ, it has been a tremendous journey of discovering God's true love for me. When I look back, I realize that this was the best decision I ever made for my life. I finally found what I was looking for. My Heavenly father has indeed made himself known to me. Each day, with the help of the Holy Spirit, and divine inspiration from the Book of Mormon, my faith has grown.

Since I met the missionaries, my prayer life has improved *for I understand that, I am just a prayer away from God.*

God has faithfully made known to me His mysteries. I have been blessed with the company of the Holy Spirit in my daily life. His goodness has been manifested in my studies, my family and my social life too. I know that my Father in heaven loves me so much. I know that I am in the right place, the true Church of Jesus Christ. I know that He spoke to Joseph Smith and still speaks to us through his prophet Thomas S.

Monson today. It is by his love for us that the priesthood keys have been restored. God has assured me that if I live in the inspiration from the Book of Mormon, obey His commandments and the priesthood, I shall have a happy life and shall live with Him eternally. My prayer is that my family too will come to bear the same testimony as I do. Amen.

From China to Washington, D.C.

We were able to teach an investigator from Washington D.C. She was originally from China, but moved to the United States to continue her education. She did not have much of a religious upbringing in China, and being in the United States introduced her to many new beliefs. She noticed that although many of the religions proclaimed to follow Jesus Christ, their actions proved otherwise. She had a Mormon friend who introduced her to the Church. The first thing that she noticed is that the members of the Church of Jesus Christ, of Latter Day Saints, not only professed that they followed Jesus Christ, but their actions showed that they were followers of Jesus Christ. She desired to learn more so her friend tried to get a Book of Mormon for her. It's not known exactly what happened but after about a month, she decided to send in a request for a Book of Mormon for herself, as well as a request for the missionaries to visit her.

She sent out the Book of Mormon request but as she was filling out the request on mormon.org for missionaries to visit her, we called to check the address. She was very surprised at how quickly we responded. After talking for a bit, we sent out the request to the local missionaries and clarified that she didn't need to send out the missionary visit request and they would come by and drop off the Book of Mormon to her home. We set up another time for us to teach her and we contacted the local missionaries to let them know that she is very interested in learning about the gospel of Jesus Christ.

As we were teaching her, the spirit was very strong, she learned a lot from our teachings and from the teachings of the local missionaries. Her heart was very open and accepting to the gospel. She said that the things she had learned from us, "seemed right and made sense," she noticed that some of the things she had done in the past was not right and that she wanted to change further, which lead to her desire to learning about the gospel. She noticed how reading the Book of Mormon and learning about the gospel of Jesus Christ brought such peace and joy into her life. My companion and I could really tell the difference that it was making in her life as we taught her day to day, She met with missionaries for seven days straight after we first contacted her and she was baptized in three weeks. She loved learning about the gospel and the people at church.

    Today, she is still a member of the Church of Jesus Christ of Latter Day Saints, and is now married to a member of the Church who has two children. She is happily living the gospel and learning more and more about the Church every day. She is working hard and striving to raise her children up in the gospel. She is excited to go to the temple and eventually be sealed to her husband and children for time and all eternity. She is excited to share the gospel with her parents who live in China, in any way possible. Her desire to share the joy and happiness she has found from the gospel of Jesus Christ after joining the Church is amazing.

The story you have just read comes from Elder Arndt.

From London, England

It was late one night and my companion and I were taking chats. As we took them, we came across a young lady from London who had some questions about The Church of Jesus Christ of Latter-day Saints. She met someone who was a member of the Church and she wanted to understand what, they believed. She had heard a lot of things about the "Mormons" but she wanted to hear about our faith from the source. So we chatted a little bit about our basic beliefs and then asked her if she would like to meet over some type of social media. She said she would love to and decided *Skype* would work best.

My companion and I were about to call her the next day. You never know just what you might encounter when you call someone over *Skype*. We called and got a bit of a surprise. Her chat was very calm and normal but as soon as we started talking we found out that this woman was very bubbly and happy! She loved to talk and loved life. We talked quite a bit the first lesson just about her life and some of her experiences and did not get into any of the lessons. She is a dancer and teaches dance to people. She had a lot of questions about our church and practices. Her friends had told her quite a bit about our faith and a lot of it was some of the typical things people have heard about The Church of Jesus Christ of Latter-day Saints. She heard that we do not use technology among many other things. So we discussed that for a bit and she was very interested to hear more. She knew a lot of what she heard could not be true because she met someone who was a Latter-day Saint and they did not fit the information.

It took us three times meeting with her to get through the first lesson because of how much she loved to talk and the questions she asked. It was great! She had a strong determination to learn and she had so much faith to begin with.

We talked about the first vision and she loved it. We asked her to watch the movie, "Joseph Smith: Prophet of the Restoration." She watched it and she told us she cried through the whole thing. Her faith just kept growing after that but that night she said she believed Joseph Smith saw what he said he did.

We asked her to attend church but she could not that Sunday but she did during the week. She met a senior couple serving a mission in London, who showed her around and introduced her to the sister missionaries in the area. During that meeting she again cried because of everything she was feeling. She started to meet with the sister missionaries as well as us. She continued to bloom in faith and was awesome to teach.

She did well with the other lessons and felt the Spirit very strongly through them. She started to go to church every week and continued to read the Book of Mormon every day. She has had some challenges in her life but she has faced everything she has with faith. She was truly an example to me and she continues to be one. She has so much love for everyone she meets and is able to show that love. She truly has the pure love of Christ and that has helped her receive the restored gospel. She was baptized just a couple of months after we first met her.

She is now organizing a temple trip for her ward and her faith is as strong as ever!

The preceding story is from Elder Bunker.

From Virginia, USA

Toward the beginning of my mission we were given a member referral and we contacted him and set up a time to meet. The first time that we talked and taught him the restoration he

Online Missionaries

wasn't very open with us but seemed to understand everything and accepted a baptismal date to work towards. We continued teaching and helping him and we noticed that he was having trouble keeping commitments such as contacting the local missionaries. We gave him a break and didn't talk for about a week. We contacted his local missionaries and found out that they could teach over *Skype* so we set that up with him and the local missionaries and it worked. He met with them over *Skype* and then progressed to meeting with them in person. Everything changed for him as he attended church. When he went to church he loved it and found out that his bishop actually lived close to him, which was a big help as well. We set another baptismal date to work towards and one day we got a message that he knew the Book of Mormon was true and that he was going to read the whole thing before he was baptized. He did complete this task and he has such an amazing testimony of the Book of Mormon and the power that is behind it. He was baptized on the second baptismal date that we set with him and we had the wonderful opportunity to *Skype* in and see, his baptism. Since his baptism, he has been able to receive the priesthood, teach in Elders quorum, and go to the temple and feel of the blessings inside and the love that his Heavenly Father has for him. You can see and trace the change in him back to going to church and reading the Book of Mormon and since then his life has been so much greater. Our first contact with this young man was in December of 2016 and he was baptized on March 11 of 2017.

The story you have just read is from Elder Woodruff.

A Note About *Skype*

By using *Skype*, you will be able to see and

talk to someone in many parts of the world for free. All you will need is a computer or an electronic device with a camera. Then simply download the free Skype app and you will be on your way. Google chat also offers a free app.

From New Zealand to Australia

One day early on in my mission, my companion and I were busy taking the chats coming in through Mormon.org. As we did so, up came a chat in the queue. One of us eagerly clicked on the chat icon, and the chat box came up so we could talk with the person on the other end. It was a young woman, from Brisbane, Australia. My companion and I engaged in conversation with her, and soon learned that her boyfriend was a member of the Church, and she had also become interested. We said we would be glad to teach her more about the Church, and she agreed to talk with us more over *Skype.* We set up a return appointment, and looked forward to talking with her again later on.

When we did, we had a great time meeting with her over *Skype.* After my companion and I shared our introductions, it was her turn. She told us of how she grew up in New Zealand, and eventually moved to Australia with her family. Not long after that, her dad and brother passed away. As she was telling this, and explained how hard it was, she was overcome with emotion and began to cry. As I listened, I felt tears well up in my eyes, and I started to mourn with her. In the midst of telling her about the Spirit World with my companion, I said, "I'm really sorry you lost your dad and your brother, but we can promise you, you will see them again." My companion gave similar words of comfort in the calm style he has, and by the end of the visit, I could tell our new investigator was uplifted, and wanted to keep learning more.

From that point, things progressed well. Our investigator was very kind and attentive, and she was always eager to learn more. She was able to go to church and engage in more church activities with her boyfriend. We told her of the Restoration of the Gospel in our next visit, and the coming forth of the Book of Mormon. She had interest in it quickly, and wanted to ask us how to study it. We gave her some tips, and did what we could to help some more. We were not really able to meet with her over *Skype* again for a while, but faithfully kept in touch, and heard that she was meeting with local missionaries, to learn more about the gospel, and the commandments. My companion and I always were happy to message her, and see how things were going. About a month later, it was pretty clear she was going to get baptized.

And so it was: In late February of 2016, she was ready for baptism, and things were all set up. At that time, she was able to *Skype* us, just before the baptism. We communicated for about fifteen minutes or so, asking how everything was going to turn out, and to congratulate her. Our investigator was shining and beaming, and I was overjoyed to see her so happy, and ready to make that promise with Heavenly Father. We retired for the night after the visit, so excited that the baptism was happening, and that we had helped this wonderful young woman reach this point in her life, to enter the waters of baptism.

The following day, we saw that we had been tagged in a Facebook post, posted by our investigator. The picture showed her with her boyfriend and an older man in white, outside an amazing church building in Australia. They all were smiling, and looked very happy and at peace. Underneath the picture, our investigator put the words, "The first day of the rest of my life." My companion and I were overjoyed. We could now see that our investigator had been baptized, and we could not be happier for her. She had made a decision that would **change her life forever** and though I have not heard much from her since, I am confident that she is living a good life, because of what she decided to do, and who she decided to be: a disciple of Christ. I am so grateful to have been a part of this, and will always remember it.

The above story is from Elder Zaugg.

From Odda, to Bergen Norway

It was the close of a very busy first day in the mission field, and I could hardly believe that I had already spoken with so many people through mormon.org. There came one chat towards the end of the day from Norway, and it was a chat that has stuck with me for the past six months of my mission. This poor young woman came on talking about how she didn't know if she even had a testimony anymore. She was going to school in Odda, Norway, which just so happened to be five hours away from the nearest church. This left her and her beliefs foreign in a world that didn't stand for what she believed in. She told us that she had been looking into the Church for a very long time, and wanted to get baptized, but her distance from church made things next to impossible for her to do anything. She was in a spot where she didn't see much hope, *but as missionaries we knew it was our duty to be there to help.*

    We continued to keep in touch with her through *Skype,* where we helped her to continue to rediscover her testimony and press on in her schooling. After having researched the Church for two and a half years, it was slightly difficult to continually find new things to talk about, *so we got creative.* This young woman was studying social work in college, and as she was fairly close to graduating at the time, there were internships opening up around the country, and there just so happened to be an opening in Bergen. *I can't say how many prayers were said in behalf of her situation.* We got a dreadful message saying that she didn't want to believe in God anymore because with her being rejected for her internship the world just seemed like too dark of a place for her. We encouraged her to say a prayer about it, and as she prayed *my companion and I prayed harder than ever before.* We came to find out later in the evening that there had been a mistake and that this woman was leaving for Bergen quicker than we had expected.

After arriving in Bergen, this woman flourished in the gospel. It was like bringing a wilting flower into the light, and her very countenance changed as she continued to progress in the gospel. After having lived her beliefs alone for a while, she was freed by no longer feeling alone. Her internship has consisted of working with a Christian Suicide Hotline service, and has occupied her time all throughout her nights. To cope with this, she fell into the habit of coffee drinking for a while. This is something that has slowed things down for her a little, but she continues to work hard for her upcoming baptism. After looking into the Church for three years, she will be baptized within the next month.

To watch someone like this fruitfully grow into all you know they can be is the best part of missionary service, as this wonderful woman has helped me to see. Just seeing her smile now is enough to brighten any dark day, because being there to make that difference is what being a missionary is all about.

The story you have just read is from Elder Curtis.

The preceding story is not just another missionary story about someone finding the gospel. To begin with, this is a story about Online Missionaries. Elder Curtis and his companion were never able to see the young woman they were teaching the gospel to in person. They could only speak to her half way around the world on the Internet and see her by using, *Skype.* The missionaries who lived this story have accomplished a modern day miracle. Do you know how difficult it can be to get an internship in the very part of the world you wish to be? In his own words, Elder Curtis said, "So we got creative." The missionaries decided to think outside of the box, to not do that which was routine and ordinary. The missionaries you have just read about prayed for the person they were trying to help and they invited her to pray for herself. Elder Curtis said, "I can't say how many prayers were said in behalf of her situation." That is because the Online Missionaries prayed too many times to count them. Jesus said, "Ask and it shall be given you, seek, and ye shall find; knock, and it shall be opened unto you: For every one that asketh receiveth; and he that seeketh findeth; and to him that knocketh, it shall be opened" (Matthew 7:7-8).

If you don't ask, how can you expect to find the answers you seek? The first story from this chapter includes the testimony of another young woman originally from China. She said, "I learned that God was only a prayer away." I like that statement because it is true.

These missionaries came up with a possible solution to this young woman's problem and they followed through with it. These online missionaries found an internship for this young woman. That was the inspiration they received after praying about the problem. They then invited this young woman to pray for herself and she did. The missionaries stayed with the problem until it was solved. This is a modern day miracle and it should be thought of as such.

This story proves that our beloved Father in heaven is aware of all his children. The Father of us all knows us all. He loves each one of us with a love we can scarcely comprehend in this life. God asks very little of each of us. He asks us to believe in his Only begotten Son, and come unto him and keep his commandments and endure until the end. And what do we get if we do that? We will be given all that the Father has.

Here are the words of the apostle Paul: "The Spirit itself beareth withness with our spirit, that we are the children of God: And if children then heirs; heirs of God, and joint-heirs with Christ; if so be that we suffer with him, that we might also be glorified together" (Romans 8:16-17).

Paul understood that we can become, "joint-heirs with Jesus Christ and heirs of God and that we can, if we live for it, eventually inherit all the Father has." What greater blessing could anyone ask for?

Chapter Thirty-Four

Be Baptized and Receive the Gift of the Holy Ghost

"And the Father Said: Repent ye, repent ye, and be baptized in the name of my Beloved Son. And also the voice of the Son came unto me, saying: He that is baptized in my name, to him will the Father give the Holy Ghost, like unto me: wherefore, follow me, and do the things which ye have seen me do" (3 Nephi 31:11-12).

I was baptized, when I was twelve years old by a well-meaning minister, of a certain Christian church. I was not given, the gift of the Holy Ghost by that minister. The Holy Ghost was not even spoken of by him. The trouble is, my baptism in that particular church was not and is not recognized by God. How do I know? The man who founded that church was Roger Williams.

The original church he founded was in Providence, Rhode Island. But he walked away from it because he said there was: "No regularly constituted church on earth, nor any person authorized to administer any Church ordinance, nor could there be until, new apostles are sent by the great Head of the Church, for whose coming, he is seeking" (Picturesque America, or the Land We Live In, ed. William Cullen Bryant, New York: D. Appleton and Co., 1872, vol. 1, p. 502).

By What Priesthood Do You Operate?

     A fair question to ask the ministers, and preachers and evangelists and priests and Rabbis of the world is this: "By what priesthood do you operate?" Do you have the Aaronic Priesthood or do you have the Melchizedek Priesthood? When they answer that they have neither the Aaronic nor the Melchizedek Priesthood one must also ask: "Then how can you expect God to recognize the things you do if you do not have the authority of God to act in his name?"

     Operating a church without the authority of God is like driving a car without a driver's license. Performing the ordinances of the holy priesthood without the keys of the holy priesthood is like hotwiring a car instead of using the car key to start it. Meanwhile none of the ordinances of God; performed by man's supposed authority alone, will be recognized by God on earth or in heaven.

Well did our Savior answer young Joseph Smith who knelt before him in the sacred grove and prayed to know which of all the churches he should join? Jesus said, "I forbid you to join any of them because: "they draw near to me with their lips and their mouths do honor me but their hearts are far from me" (Matthew 15:18). And because they follow the precepts of men, they will fulfill the prophecy of the Apostle Paul wherein he said they will be: "Ever learning and never able to come to a knowledge of the truth" (2 Timothy 3:7).

Whence Cometh the Authority to Baptize?

"We believe that a man must be called of God, by prophesy, and by the laying of hands, by those who are in authority to preach the Gospel and administer in the ordinances thereof"(The fifth Article of Faith of The Church of Jesus Christ of Latter-day Saints). You cannot get God's authority by graduating from a university or a seminary. You cannot buy the authority of God to administer the ordinances of God with money. There was a certain man named Simon in the days following the crucifixion of our Savior who offered Peter money that he might have the power to place his hands on people's heads and give them the gift of the Holy Ghost, which power Peter and the other apostles had. But Peter said to Simeon, "Thy money perish with thee, because thou hast thought to buy the gift of God with money" (Acts 8:20).

The authority to act in God's name comes to a man when he is worthy. Faith in Christ, repentance, baptism, the gift of the Holy Ghost and enduring until the end is required. A broken heart and a contrite spirit, is also required.

How were you baptized? Were you sprinkled? That will not do. You must be baptized the way the Son of God was baptized. We read from the Book of Matthew, "And Jesus when he was baptized went up straightway out of the water: and lo, the heavens were opened unto him, and he saw the Spirit of God descending like a dove, and lighting upon him" (Matthew 3:16). All must be baptized the way our Savior was baptized by John the Baptist. One must be fully immersed under the water and then come up out of the water.

Were you baptized by someone-who has the authority of God to baptize? Were you given the gift of the Holy Ghost by one who has the authority of God to give you the gift of the Holy Ghost? Those are not hard questions to ask but they may be hard truths to accept until the Holy Ghost steps in and reveals the truth to you.

Concerning the importance of baptism by water and the gift of the Holy Ghost the Lord has said: "For by the water ye are justified and by the blood ye are sanctified" (Moses 6: 60). Then the Lord continued to speak to us about the Holy Ghost: "Therefore it is given to abide in you; the record of heaven; the Comforter, the peaceable things of immortal glory; the truth of all things; that which quickeneth all things; which maketh alive all things; that which knoweth all things and hath all power according to wisdom, mercy, truth, justice and judgment" (Moses 6:61). And that is the marvelous endowment of the Holy Ghost. Every man and woman should seek Him out to be their constant companion while they live on earth.

It was the Holy Ghost who took the man Adam in his arms and baptized him when there was no other man on earth who had the authority to do that. (Moses 6:64-68). It was the Holy Ghost who carried Nephi to an exceeding high mountain and allowed Nephi to see with his own eyes that the Holy Ghost was a spirit in the form of a man. (1 Nephi 11:1). It was the Holy Ghost who carried Phillip away after Phillip baptized the eunuch following the crucifixion of the Savior. (Acts 8:34-40).

Be Baptized and Receive the Gift of the Holy Ghost

It will be the Holy Ghost who will baptize you with fire and with the gift of the Holy Ghost if you will prepare yourself for baptism, albeit a mortal man who will have the authority of God to lay his hands upon your head and speak the words of the ordinance, it will be the Holy Ghost who will come upon you and dwell in you and not tarry with you. Then after you have been given the gift of the Holy Ghost, he will be your constant companion if you will continue to love God and keep his commandments and endure until the end. There is no greater gift a man could have until our Savior returns. The Holy Ghost will lift us, guide us, teach and instruct us, and bring peace and hope and inspiration to us until the Savior returns.

The Holy Ghost is a wonderful companion to have. We know precious little about him. We know that the Holy Ghost is a member of the supreme presidency of the Gods. He is therefore, a member of the Godhead. We do not know if the Holy Ghost is also a spirit son of God the Eternal Father as is our beloved Savior. The Father has not yet revealed from whence the Holy Ghost came. We know only that the Holy Ghost is a spirit in the form of a man, pertaining to his personal identity. Thus, he has not yet taken upon himself a physical body. But oh, what marvelous powers and gifts of the spirit he has been given! Although the Holy Ghost can only be in one place at one time, he has the wonderful capacity to spread the influence of his spirit of light and truth throughout all of time and space. The Holy Ghost is the ultimate friend, and companion to seek after until our beloved Savior returns to the earth.

The Aaronic Priesthood

Concerning the authority to baptize: John the Baptist, "was ordained by the angel of God at the time he was eight days old" D&C 84:28). John the Baptist was born to pave the way of the Savior and to baptize the Son of God. Jesus said of John the Baptist, "Among those that are born of women there is not a greater prophet than John the Baptist: but he who is least in the kingdom of heaven is greater than he" (Luke 7:28).

Many wise men have said, "Know thyself." Of all the men to have lived besides Jesus Christ, John the Baptist knew who he was, and why? Because the Holy Ghost was instructing him and teaching him from the time he was in his mother's womb! John the Baptist dressed, "in camel's hair and ate locusts and wild honey with a girdle of skin about his loins" (Mark 1:6). John the Baptist and Jesus were cousins. John the Baptist knew his limitations. He knew he had not power to give the Holy Ghost and made that clear to those who asked him.

John The Baptist Has Returned to the Earth to Restore the Aaronic Priesthood

John the Baptist has returned to the earth as an angel of God to restore the Aaronic priesthood, which holds the keys of baptism by immersion for the remission of sins. The prophet Joseph Smith has recorded: "Two days after the arrival of Mr. Cowdery (being the 7th of April, I commenced to translate the Book of Mormon, and he began to write for me. We still continued the work of translation, when in the ensuing month (May, 1829), we on a certain day went into the woods to pray and inquire of the Lord respecting baptism for the remission of sins, that we found mentioned in the translation of the plates.

While we were thus employed, praying and calling upon the Lord, a messenger from heaven descended in a cloud of light, and having laid his hands upon us, he ordained us, saying: Upon you my fellow servants, in the name of

Messiah, I confer the Priesthood of Aaron, which holds the keys of the ministering of angles, and of the gospel of repentance, and of baptism by immersion for the remission of sins; and this shall never be taken again from the earth until the sons of Levi do offer again an offering unto the Lord in righteousness. He said this Aaronic Priesthood had not the power of laying on of hands for the gift of the Holy Ghost, but that this should be conferred on us hereafter; and he commanded us to go and be baptized, and gave us directions that I should baptize Oliver Cowdery, and that afterwards he should baptize me. The messenger who visited us on this occasion and conferred this Priesthood upon us, said that his name was John, the same that is called John the Baptist in the New Testament and that he acted under the direction of Peter, James, and John, who held the keys of the Priesthood of Melchizedek which Priesthood, he said, would in due time be conferred on us, and that I should be called the first Elder of the Church, and he (Oliver Cowdery) the second. It was on the fifteenth day of May, 1829 that we were ordained under the hand of this messenger and baptized" (Joseph Smith 2:67-72).

    Therefore, as of May fifteenth 1829 the authority of God to baptize by immersion for the remission of sins has been restored to the earth.

The Melchizedek Priesthood

When Jesus organized his church upon the earth, he called his chosen twelve apostles to stand before him and he then ordained them as apostles and especial witnesses of Jesus Christ. Speaking of his twelve chosen apostles, Jesus said, "Ye have not chosen me but I have chosen you, and ordained you, that ye should go and bring forth fruit, and that your fruit should remain: that whatsoever ye ask the Father in my name, he may give it you" (John 15:16). The apostle Paul explained that no man could give the holy priesthood to himself: "No man taketh this honor unto himself, but he that is called of God as was Aaron. So also Christ glorified not himself to be made an high priest; but he that saith unto him, Thou art my Son, today have I begotten thee" (Hebrews 5:4-6). The higher or Melchizedek Priesthood comes from God and not from man and it must be conferred upon man: by God.

Peter, James and John Have Restored the Melchizedek Priesthood in Our Day

Peter, James and John have visited the earth as angels of God to restore the Melchizedek Priesthood, which holds the keys to give the gift of the Holy Ghost by the laying on of hands. The scripture says: "And also with Peter, and James, and John, whom I have sent unto you, by whom I have ordained you and confirmed you to be apostles and especial witnesses of my name, and bear the keys of your ministry and of the same things which I revealed unto them; Unto whom I have committed the keys of my kingdom, and a dispensation of my gospel for the last times, and for the fullness of times, in which I will gather together in one all things, both which are in heaven, and which are on the earth; And also with all those whom my Father hath given me out of the world" (D&C 27:12-14).

Once again, without the authority to act in the name of God, one cannot perform any ordinance of the holy priesthood or do any other thing in the name of God and expect God to recognize whatever it is you do!

When you are baptized for the remission of sins, you will go down under the water. When you come up, out of the water, if you have truly repented of your sins before your baptism, your

Be Baptized and Receive the Gift of the Holy Ghost

sins are literally washed away and you become a new person in Christ.

When we receive the gift of the Holy Ghost there is a dynamic change in us. We can now be able to see things and feel things and understand spiritual things that we have not been able to see, feel, and understand before. The gift of the Holy Ghost can now guide us in all the ways of light and truth. I have seen the gift of the Holy Ghost working. I have felt the gift of the Holy Ghost working. I have heard the whisperings of the still small voice (which is the Holy Ghost) in my mind and in my heart. It is real.

When you are baptized and receive the gift of the Holy Ghost you will have taken that all important step in your eternal progression. Now, the gate that leads to eternal life will open for you and you will be on that straight and narrow path that will lead you to the kingdom of heaven. Now you will be on your way to not just changing your life which can be very temporary and change with the whims and fads of man but you will now be on your way to **changing your life for the better forever!**

The End

Epilogue

No Sacrifice, No Blessing

Following more than a year of observing him, I noticed that one of my dear friends who serves with me in the temple was always the first one there, sitting quietly and waiting for our prayer and preparation meeting which began at 5:15 AM. I arrived early myself and on one day I thought to myself, I'll beat him there today, so I arrived a 4:30 AM but when I walked in, he was sitting there quietly waiting as usual. I knew that when he finished serving there, he would go to his workplace where he worked for 10 hours. Just recently, he told me that on his day off he would be baptizing four people that he helped to teach the gospel to in his neighborhood. Some full-time missionaries struggle for their entire two-year missions to accomplish that. He informed me that he was also serving as the ward mission leader. His bishop brings many young people from his ward with him to the temple baptistery every other Saturday morning. On one occasion, I asked my friend, how is it you can arrive so early and still manage to work for 10 hours and even find the time to help the full-time missionaries teach the gospel? I have shared his story and his answer several times since he gave them to me. He said: *"No Sacrifice, No Blessing."*

That seems to be what so many of us are missing when we look for blessings. We are very good at praying for the blessings and we even believe that the blessings will come but we seem to leave just one thing out of the equation. We fail to offer our sacrifice to God. In Old Testament times the sacrifice required was the firstlings of ones flocks, a lamb without spot and without blemish. (See, Exodus 12:5-7). This was symbolic of the sacrifice of our beloved Savior who by and through his infinite atonement, redeemed man from the fall of Adam. The apostle Peter has written:

"Forasmuch as ye know that ye were not redeemed with corruptible things, as silver and gold, from your vain conversation received by tradition from your fathers: *But with the precious blood of Jesus Christ, as of a lamb without blemish and without spot.*

Who verily was foreordained before the foundation of the world, but was manifest in these last times for you" (1 Peter 1 18-20).

But that has changed. Before we continue with that however, let us consider this: Arriving early shows ones faithfulness and commitment. It also demonstrates that a person is dependable.

Being early is a wonderful habit to get into. I was taught as a young missionary to always be 15 minutes early for all, important meetings. That habit has stayed with me throughout my life. I have been able to read many books while arriving early and waiting for doctor's and dentist appointments for example. When I arrive early, I always bring a book to read with me, or a project I am working on. However, it takes more than just being early to change ones heart, and that is what you want to be able to accomplish if you hope to change your life for the better forever.

Allow Your Heart to Change

How do you get to the place in your life when you find yourself wanting to help others, to serve others, to minister to others? Answer. You begin to allow your own heart to change. You become childlike. Children are innocent and pure. Children are teachable. Become teachable, like a little child. Many grown-ups think they know all the answers. In reality, no one does.

Realize that we are all still learning, just like a child.

Then ask God to give you a new heart, one that will cause you to desire to help build up His kingdom in heaven and on the earth. That is our Heavenly Father's mission statement. The Lord has said: "This is my work and my glory, to bring to pass the immortality and eternal life of man" (Moses 1:39). When one begins to understand this, he will seek to help God accomplish his desire for all of his children and that is, that they may all be worthy to return to live with him in heaven and enjoy eternal life.

The Lord has given all of his sons and daughters instructions for how to behave in our day: *"Thou shalt offer a sacrifice unto the Lord thy God in righteousness, even that of a broken heart and a contrite spirit" (D&C 59:9).*

A broken heart is just that, it is a submissive heart. It is a heart that is teachable. A contrite spirit is a spirit that is meek and lowly. It is a spirit that is humble and yes, teachable. Arrogance and pride have no part here, they are not characteristic of one who possesses a broken heart and a contrite spirit. Such a person does not stir up contention and wrath. Such a person is slow to anger and speaks softly. Such a person shares his witness of Jesus Christ often and reaches out to help, serve and minister to others.

Such a person does not boast of himself but praises and lifts others up.

When I read the scripture above, I want to let go of anger. I want to stop judging people and look for the good in everyone. I want to point out their good qualities and share them with others.

You can change your life forever. You can prepare yourself to be worthy to enter heaven when your life comes to an end. You may wish to do this for your own family and loved ones and not merely for yourself. Remember, families can be together forever when this life ends. The necessary steps have been spelled out many times throughout this book.

Why not decide to do this now? Find a quiet place where you can get down on your knees and talk to God. Ask God to help you to prepare yourself and decide that you will do whatever it takes, to assure your own heart before God that all is well with you. Ask God to help you get your life in order. The first step will always be to admit that you have sinned. Then you must decide to change. Remember, God's word for change is the word, *repent.* Decide that you will repent of your old ways. Ask God to help you and he will.

Now comes perhaps the most crucial step of all that you must do. So crucial to entering the kingdom of God that Jesus set the example for all of mankind by doing this one thing himself. Decide that you will be baptized. The ordinance of baptism will allow the gate to eternal life to open for you.

Once you are baptized you will be able to stand on the other side of that gate and walk down that straight and narrow path to eternal life. When you receive the gift of the Holy Ghost, God's promise to you is clear. The Holy Ghost will then teach you all things that you should do until the Savior returns to the earth. Then, if you will endure to the end, the Father has promised, "you shall have eternal life."

When you do these things you will become a new creature in Christ. Life will forever change for you. You will quickly learn that, "it is impossible not to get better with Christ in your life." You will now have the desire to help others to gain the same knowledge of spiritual truths as you now have. You will soon learn the meaning of the Lord's new invitation to you: "When thou art converted, strengthen thy brethren"(Luke 22:32).

The gospel of Jesus Christ can be defined nicely with but a few short verses of scripture. They are: "By this shall all men know that ye are my disciples, If ye have love one to another" (John 13:35). Jesus taught: "But whosoever will be great among you, let him be your minister;

And whosoever will be chief among you, let him be your servant" (Matthew 20:26-27).

I promise you this: If you will love one another and serve one another and minister to the needs of others, you will quickly, Change Your Life Forever!

Epilogue #2

Share the Gospel with All the World

The number of people living on earth as of June 2017 is approximately, 7.5 billion" (From Wikipedia).

The earth. Photo taken from space. (From Wikipedia).

Our beloved Savior has given his followers a mandate to take the gospel of Jesus Christ to all men and women who live on the earth: *"Go ye therefore, and teach all nations, baptizing them in the name of the Father, and of the Son, and of the Holy Ghost. Teaching them to observe all things whatsoever I have commanded you: and, lo, I am with you always, eve unto the end of the world. Amen"* (Matthew 28: 19-20).

How can we possibly do this? The answer is: It cannot be done: by the missionaries on their own. It will be accomplished by allowing those who wish to learn about the gospel of Jess Christ to contact us and by you and me sharing the gospel with everyone we can. The Online Missionaries are one way we will reach every nation; kindred, tongue and people. This is the future and the future is here now!

The Lord has called missionaries to serve their missions in 150 countries of the world as of 2017. There are currently seventeen Online Missionaries serving at the MTC in Provo, Utah. They have had 37 baptisms by June of this year (2017). Their goal for the year 2017 is 70 convert baptisms. This is just the beginning.

No matter what country of the world you live in, don't worry about someone on the other end of the line being able to speak your particular language and understand you. There are presently, 56 languages being taught at the Missionary Training Center in Provo, Utah.

People Living in the Following Countries Have Contacted the Online Missionaries Serving At the MTC in Provo, Utah

1. United States of America 2. Australia 3. Japan
4. Germany 5. Peru 6. Netherlands 7. Finland
8. Canada 9. Czech Republic 10.Italy 11.Belgium
12. Sri Lanka 13. Philippines 14. Ghana
15. South Africa 16. India 17. United Kingdom
18. Scotland 19. Ireland 20. Mauritius 21.Poland
22. Chile 23. Sweden 24. Greece 25. Cyprus
26. Latvia 27. Mexico 28. France 29. Norway
30. Hungary 31. Slovenia 32. Bulgaria 33.Turkey
34. Albania 35. Denmark 36. Nigeria
37. Myanmar 38. Fiji 39. Kenya 40. Jamaica
41. Romania 42. New Zealand 43. Croatia
44. El Salvador 45. Portugal 46. New Guinea
47. Trinidad and Tobago 48. Macedonia
49. Suriname 50. Costa Rica 51. Hawaii
52. South Korea 53. Zambia 54. Pakistan
55. Ethiopia 56. Gambia 57. Thailand
58. French Polynesia 59. Haiti 60. Columbia
61. Guyana 62. Morocco 63. Liberia 64. Namibia
65. Samoa 66. Brazil 67. Argentina 68. F. Guyana
69. Armenia 70. Guatemala 71. Belize

72. Russia 73. Taiwan 74. Dominican Republic
75. Indonesia 76. Puerto Rico 77. Panama
78. U.S. Virgin Islands 79. Nicaragua
80. Mauritania 81. Georgia 82. Côte D'Ivoire
83. Egypt 84. Singapore 85. Afghanistan
86. Burundi 87. Tonga 88. Lithuania
89. Cape Verde 90. Kosovo 91. Madagascar
92. Mozambique 93. Uganda 94. Ecuador
95. Austria 96. 97. Uruguay 98. Botswana
99. Venezuela 100. Tanzania 101. Paraguay
102. Kiribati 103. Kiribas 104. China
105. The Bahamas 106. Cameroon 107. Iran
108. Guam (From the MTC in Provo, Utah).

As of August of 2017 there are presently, 192 countries on planet earth. (From Wikipedia). That still leaves forty-two countries of the world and billions of people to hear the everlasting gospel and come unto Christ and change their lives forever!

What can you do to help? First of all, get yourself converted! Then, do not just fast and pray for the missionaries serving all over the world but get out there and help. There are endless opportunities around you. Talk to those you feel led to. Get out there and make a difference. Get out there and be a missionary!

About the Author

Ronald H. Bartalini was born and raised in California. He is the author of five inspirational and motivational books. He has published three children's picture books, "Hoppity Moose and the Red Caboose," "The Little Leaf Tree," and "Happy Monsters" with "Prince Galem and the Golden Key" soon to be published. He has also written four books of poetry. "My Greatest Love, Missionary Stories from My Life" has made its way to 24 countries of the world so far.

Index

A

Aaronic, 304-305
Acknowledge the hand of God, 67
Adversary, 168-174
Agency, 97-98
Angels, 302; 305
Anger, 171
Apostles and prophets, 305-306; 309
Ask, 79-80; 94; 178
Attitude Adjustment, 63-64
Atonement, 114-120; 149; 187; 309
Authority, 298-302

B

Baptism, 298-301; 303-304; 306; 313
Bible, 190-193
Book of Mormon, 83; 94-95; 232-240
Broken heart, 189; 299

C

Change of heart, 69
Chief among you, 314
Comforter, 77
Compliments, 59-60

Condemn the world, 126
Contention, 117
Contrite spirit, 189
Correction, 63
Creator, 144

D

Devil, 168-174
Distractions, 269
Dostoyevsky, 234-235

E

Elder Guo's conversion story, 81-88
Endure, 224
Eternal life, 212
Evil, Chapter 18
Excuses, 51; Chapters 19-25

F

Faith, 215; 241
Faith in Christ, 241-251
Fast, the law of, 258-259
Firstborn, 147
First Man, 106; 161
First great commandment, 262

G

Garden of Eden, 106-107
Gifts of the Spirit, 164-167
Gift of the Holy Ghost, 218
Glory, 147
Gospel of Jesus Christ, 225; 227-231; 313-314
Grace, 187; 121-122
Grain of mustard seed, 50
Great among you, 313

H

Holy Ghost, 152-153; 314
Honor, 67; 170; 299

I

Infinite atonement, 110; 114-120; 187; 318
Intelligence, xvi; 158
Invitation to Come Unto Christ, 265-267

J

Jesus Christ, 140-151
Joint heirs with Christ, 159; 295
John the Baptist, 302-304
Judge not, 53-54

K

Kingdom of God, 74

L

Languages spoken in the world today, 191
Law of Moses, 231
Liar from the beginning, 174
Light of the body, 103
Light of Christ, 96-103
Light of the world, 97
Light, true light, 97
Love, xv; 96, 213-214; 216
Lucifer, 168-169; 173

M

Man of holiness, 157
Melchizedek, 305-307
Mercy, 188
Millions of earths, 157
Minister to the needs of others, 313-314
Miracles, 130-134
Missionaries, 269
Missionaries, number serving, 268
Moral compass, 70
Murderer from the beginning, 174

N

Natural man or Physical man, 160-161
Naysayers, 49-50
Number of Bible translations, 190-191
Number of Christian churches- worldwide, 195

O

Omnipotence, 300
Omnipresence, 153
Omniscience, 143
Online missionaries, 271-295
Only begotten Son, 140-141; 148
Only name given under heaven, 76; 219

P

Parables:
The parable of the Good Tree, 154-155
The parable of the Three Trees, 162-163
The parable of the Complaining and Impatient Man, 185-186
The parable of Three Selfish Strangers, 229-230
Paradise, 107
Pearl of Great Price, 138; 233

Phone numbers to contact missionaries... Within the United States:
(888) 537-7700
Outside the United States:
1-(888) 537-7700

Plan of Salvation, 75; 110-113
Prayer, 294-295
Priesthood authority, 297-302

R

Recharge, 92-95
Redeemer, 21-23; 148-149; 309
Repentance, 110; 149
Report, back to yourself, 49
Resist, things we, 50-51
Resurrection and the life, 72; 142
Rudolph the Red Nosed Reindeer, 50-51

S

Sabbath day, 260-261
Sacrifice, 145; 308-311
Sanctify, 122
Salvation, 110-113; 149
Satan, 168-174
Savior, 140-141; 146-147; 317
Second great commandment, 262
Sermon on the Mount, 98; 151
Servant, 314

Sinned, all have, 187
Son of God, 147; 301
Spirit body, 160
Spirit matter, 158-160
Spirit prison, 108-109
Spirit of truth, 121
Spirit world, 107
Songs:
Don't Hurt Worms, 212
His Religion Is Not My Religion, 194-195
Learn to Listen, 78-79

T

Talents, 150; 163
Temples, 225-226
Test to find the true Church of Christ, 252-263
Test to know good from evil, 128-129
Thank you, 64-66
Thoughts, 269
Tithing, 261
Translations of the Bible, 190-193
Truth, 206
Traditions, 203-206

W

Worthiness, 185-189

www.ingramcontent.com/pod-product-compliance
Lightning Source LLC
Chambersburg PA
CBHW051037160426
43193CB00010B/969